THE DETROIT LIONS:
Decades of New Beginnings

by
Thomas E. Hall

Also by Thomas E. Hall

Business Cycles:
The Nature and Causes of Economic Fluctuations

The Great Depression:
An International Disaster of Perverse Economic Policies
(with J.D. Ferguson)

The Rotten Fruits of Economic Controls and the Rise from the Ashes, 1965-1989

The Quadrangle

Tapper Jones

Aftermath:
The Unintended Consequences of Public Policies

Walking the Edge:
A Novel of 1920s Detroit

CONTENTS

Preface

Through the 2022 season, the Detroit Lions have won four NFL championships. Unfortunately for the team's fans the last one came in 1957. More than six decades have passed since the Lions last appeared in an NFL title game, and the team has ranked near the bottom of the league for years. Their record from 1958-2022 is 417-572-19 which is a win rate of 42 percent. In recent years it's been even worse: since 2000 the team has won 35 percent of their games.

Despite the futility, plenty of fans still support the team. One reason is simple geography: fans tend to root for teams from the area where they grew up. Over time, the bond grows strong and hard to break. Another reason is hope. Team followers have been figuratively kicked in the teeth season after season, yet they keep coming back for more because there's always that chance that it'll be different the next time around. The rallying cry of Lions' fans everywhere has long been "Maybe next year!"

This book tells the story of the post-1957 Lions. It describes significant events that took place since the last championship, the major personalities involved, and addresses reasons why the franchise has experienced so little on-field success. It also documents those occasional seasons when quality Lions' teams came close to reaching the league championship game.

Ownership has been a huge part of the problem. The Lions' declining fortunes post-1957 roughly coincide with William Clay Ford's purchase of the team in 1963. He controlled the franchise for half a century and during thirty-one of those years employed two general managers—Russ Thomas and Matt Millen—who failed to assemble winning teams. Meanwhile, coaches were hired and fired with frequency. Another problem has been player acquisition. The Lions have found stars—and a few superstars—but have been held back by the rest of the roster. The team has also suffered an inordinate amount of bad luck: any Lions' fan can tell stories about miscues at key moments—fumbles; interceptions; dropped passes; blown pass coverages; missed blocks; and missed tackles—that cost games. Another issue—often overlooked—was the decision made in the 1970s to move to an indoor stadium.

It's been a long, hard road for Detroit's football fans. Hopefully, the future will differ from the past because a new generation of ownership took control of the team in 2020. The Lions are embarked on yet another rebuilding program and the early results are encouraging.

Several people assisted on this project by reading chapter drafts and offering comments and suggestions. They are Rick Dorshow, Rich Douglas, Alex Hall, Chris Hall, Kaylyn Hall, Rich Hart, John Kantarian, Joe Moravek, and Steve Parsons. I am grateful to all of them. Any errors are my responsibility.

Detroit Lions
Timeline of Notable Events

1930 – Portsmouth (Ohio) Spartans join the National Football League.

1931 – George "Potsy" Clark becomes head coach.

1934 – George Richards buys the Spartans, moves them to Detroit, and changes their name to Lions. He schedules a home game on Thanksgiving Day, thereby starting a tradition the team has followed most every year since.

1935 – Lions win their first league title by defeating the New York Giants 26-7 in the NFL Championship Game.

1936 – Potsy Clark resigns at the end of the season and is replaced by future Hall of Fame quarterback Earl "Dutch" Clark who serves as player-coach for two seasons. Earl Clark is the first in a string of six head coaches over the next eleven seasons (including Potsy Clark who returns for the 1940 season).

1942 – Lions go winless with a record of 0-11. During the season they score 38 points (never more than 7 in one game), give up 263 points, and are shut out five times.

1943 – Lions end the season 3-6-1. The tie game occurs on November 7th at Briggs Stadium when the Lions and NY Giants play to a score of 0-0. It is the last scoreless tie in NFL history.

1950 – The Lions acquire quarterback Bobby Layne in a trade with the New York Bulldogs. Layne is with the Lions for eight-plus years, playing alongside other future Hall of Famers Jack Christensen, Lou Creekmur, Frank Gatski, John Henry Johnson, Yale Lary, Joe Schmidt, Dick Stenfel, and Doak Walker. During the decade the team appears in four NFL Championship Games.

1951 – Buddy Parker is named head coach. The Lions finish the season 7-4-1 which earns them second place in the Western Conference.

1952 – Lions' 9-3 record puts them in a tie with the Los Angeles Rams for first place in the conference. The playoff game is held in Detroit and the Lions defeat the Rams 31-12 to advance to the title against Cleveland. The Lions defeat the Browns 17-7 to win their second NFL Championship.

1953 – Lions win the Western Conference with a 10-2 record. In the title game they prevail over Cleveland 17-16 to win their third NFL Championship.

1954 – Lions lose to the Cleveland Browns 10-56 in the NFL Championship Game.

1956 – Lions end the season 9-3 and in second place in the conference.

1957 – During the preseason, Head Coach Buddy Parker resigns and is replaced by George Wilson. Bobby Layne is badly injured in the next-to-last game of the regular season and Tobin Rote takes over full-time quarterback duties. The Lions finish 8-4 which puts them in a tie with San Francisco for first place in the Western Conference. In the playoff game at San Francisco the Lions stage a 31-27 come-from-behind victory. A week later the Lions defeat the Cleveland Browns 59-14 to win their fourth NFL Championship.

1958 – Lions use their first-round draft pick to select University of Iowa defensive lineman Alex Karris. Shortly after the season begins, Bobby Layne is traded to the Pittsburgh Steelers which starts the legend of "The Curse of Bobby Layne."

1961 – The Detroit Lions' owners group elects William Clay Ford as team president.

1962 – Lions go 11-3, but come in second in the Western Conference behind the 13-1 Green Bay Packers. The Lions' three losses are by a total of eight points. They miss winning the division because of an early-season loss at Green Bay, a game the Lions seemingly have won but give away because of a bad offensive play call with less than two minutes left. The season's highlight takes place on Thanksgiving Day when the Lions hand the Packers their only loss of the season.

1963 – Alex Karras is suspended for betting on football. Writer George Plimpton participates in the Lions' training camp as a supposed candidate for third-string quarterback. His experiences provide the material for his book *Paper Lion* which is published in 1966 and made into a movie released in 1968. In November, William Clay Ford buys out the other team owners for $4.5 million.

1964 – On January 10th, William Clay Ford takes control as sole owner. After sitting out one season, Alex Karris is reinstated to play.

1967 – William Clay Ford appoints Russ Thomas as general manager and Joe Schmidt as head coach. The Lions have an exceptional draft that includes Hall of Famer Lem Barney, Mel Farr, and longtime defensive stalwarts Paul Naumoff and Mike Weger. On August 5th, in the first-ever preseason game pitting an NFL team against an AFL team, the Lions lose to the Denver Broncos. Alex Karras, who said he'd walk home from Denver if the Lions lost, takes the team flight back to Detroit.

1968 – The Lions select University of Minnesota tight end Charlie Sanders in the third round.

1970 – The Lions come on strong late in the season and post a 10-4 record which includes a loss on November 8th to the New Orleans Saints when Tom Dempsey kicks his record-breaking 63-yard field goal as time expires. The Lions earn a wild card berth in the playoffs and face the Cowboys in Dallas, but lose by a score of 0-5 in what remains the lowest scoring NFL playoff game of all time.

1971 – In February, the Lions sign an agreement with the City of Pontiac to play in a domed stadium that will be completed in 1975. During a game at Tiger Stadium on October 24th, Lions' wide receiver Chuck Hughes suffers a heart attack and collapses on the field. He is rushed to the hospital where he is declared dead.

1973 – After six years as Lions' head coach, Joe Schmidt resigns in January. Don McCafferty, who coached the Baltimore Colts to victory in Super Bowl V, is hired to replace him.

1974 – In July, Head Coach Don McCafferty dies of a heart attack. Rick Forzano is named as replacement. On Thanksgiving Day, the Lions play their last game at Tiger Stadium.

1975 – In the second-round of the NFL draft, the Lions choose University of Texas defensive lineman Doug English. Along with Al "Bubba" Baker, Dave Pureifory, and John Woodcock, English will form the core of the Lions "Silver Rush" defensive line of the late 1970s and early 1980s. Lions begin play in the Pontiac Silverdome and have a lackluster 7-7 season that includes a blowout 10-31 loss to the Dallas Cowboys in the home opener, and the 0-20 "Thanksgiving Day Massacre" at the hands of the Los Angeles Rams. On a higher note, the Lions defeat the Vikings in the final game of the season. It is one of just three Detroit victories over Minnesota during the 1970s.

1976 – Four games into the season, Head Coach Rick Forzano resigns. He is replaced by Tommy Hudspeth. The Lions post a 6-8 record.

1978 – After posting another 6-8 record in 1977, Tommy Hudspeth and his entire coaching staff are fired on January 9th. Monte Clark is named head coach. In the second round of the draft the Lions choose defensive lineman Al "Bubba" Baker of Colorado State University. His exceptional pass rushing ability earns him NFL Defensive Rookie of the Year.

1979 – Decimated by injuries, the Lions compile a 2-12 record.

1980 – Since the Lions had the worst record in 1979, they choose first in the 1980 NFL draft and select University of Oklahoma running back Billy Sims. On Thanksgiving Day the Lions blow a 17-3 lead to the Bears as Chicago scores two touchdowns in the final quarter, tying the game as time expires. The Bears win the ensuing coin flip and choose to receive the ball. Bears' running back Dave Williams returns the kickoff for a touchdown to win the game, and the 21 seconds-long overtime period goes into the record book as the shortest in NFL history. The record stands for seventeen years.

1981 – In a rare break that goes Detroit's way, the Lions defeat the Dallas Cowboys 27-24 in a nationally televised game at the Silverdome when placekicker Eddie Murray makes a 47-yard field goal as time expires. During the game-ending play the Lions have twelve men on the field but the officials don't call a penalty. In the final game of the season, the Lions meet the Buccaneers at the Silverdome to determine the Central Division winner. The Lions lose 17-20, end the season 8-8, and miss the playoffs.

1982 – In a strike-shortened season, the Lions qualify for the playoffs with a 4-5 record.

1983 – In the January playoff game at Washington, the Lions turn the ball over five times and lose 7-31. During the 1983 season the Lions start 1-4, then heat up and end the season 9-7 which is good enough to win the NFC Central Division. The playoff game takes place on New Year's Eve in San Francisco, and with seconds left and trailing by 1 point the Lions line up for a 44-

yard field goal that will win the game. Lions' placekicker Eddie Murray misses wide right.

1984 – Lions fall to 4-11-1. On October 21st in Minneapolis, Billy Sims suffers a career-ending knee injury. Monte Clark is fired on December 19th.

1985 – Darryl Rogers is named head coach. Lions use their first-round draft pick to select University of Florida offensive lineman Lomas Brown.

1987 – In what might be the Lions' worst first-round draft pick of all time, they select University of Washington defensive lineman Reggie Rogers. Due in large part to psychiatric problems, Rogers plays in just six games during his rookie year. NFL players go on strike after the second week of the season. Week 3 games are cancelled, and games played during weeks 4-6 use replacement players. The Lions post a season record of 4-11.

1988 – Lions draft University of Miami defensive back Bennie Blades in the first round. On October 20th Reggie Rogers, driving while legally intoxicated, runs a red light in downtown Pontiac and slams into a car carrying three teenage boys. All three teens are killed and Rogers suffers a broken neck. On November 14th, and with the Lions at 2-9, Head Coach Darryl Rogers is fired and assistant Wayne Fontes is elevated to interim head coach.

1989 – With the third pick in the draft, the Lions choose Oklahoma State University running back Barry Sanders. General Manager Russ Thomas retires and is replaced by Chuck Schmidt.

1991 – The Lions use their first-round pick to select University of Virginia wide receiver Herman Moore. During a November 17th game against the Rams, offensive lineman Mike Utley is permanently paralyzed when his head hits the Silverdome turf and he suffers severe injury to vertebrae in his neck. The Lions go 12-4 and win the NFC Central Division. They will host a playoff game for the first time since the 1950s.

1992 – In the divisional round game played on January 5th at the Silverdome, the Lions have their greatest moment since 1957 when they rout the Dallas Cowboys 38-6 and advance to the NFC Championship. The conference title game is played a week later in Washington and the Lions fall 10-41. The Lions use their first-round draft pick to select South Carolina State defensive lineman Robert Porcher. On May 8th, Lions' defensive backfield coach Len Fontes (brother of head coach Wayne Fontes) dies of a heart attack. On June 23rd, offensive lineman Eric Andolsek is killed when a truck veers off the road and hits him while he's working in the front yard of his home in Louisiana.

1993 – The Lions go 10-6 and win the NFC Central Division. They will host a playoff game for the second time since the 1950s.

1994 – The Packers visit the Silverdome on January 8th as a wild card team. In an exciting back-and-forth game, the Lions fall 24-28. During the 1994 season the Lions go 9-7 and make the playoffs as a wild card. On New Year's Eve they meet the Packers in Green Bay and lose 16-12. Barry Sanders is held to –1 yard rushing.

1995 – The Lions' season starts poorly, but they win the final seven games to go 10-6 and make the playoffs as a wild card. The playoff game is held in Philadelphia on December 30th, and the

Lions fall behind 7-51 before eventually losing 37-58.

1996 – On August 20th, the Lions announce their plan to build an indoor stadium in Detroit. The team posts a 5-11 record. Wayne Fontes is fired at the end of the season.

1997 – Bobby Ross is hired as head coach. Barry Sanders rushes for 2,053 yards in 335 attempts which works out to an incredible 6.1 yards per carry. The Lions go 9-7 and make the playoffs as a wild card. The playoff game is in Tampa on December 28th and the Lions lose 10-20.

1998 – In one of the most famous Thanksgiving Day games ever, the Lions and Steelers are tied at the end of regulation. During the coin toss prior to overtime play, Steelers' running back Jerome Bettis, apparently intending to call "tails", says "hea-tails" which the referee interprets as "heads." The coin comes up tails so the Lions are awarded the flip and choose to receive the kickoff. The Lions drive down the field and kick a game-winning field goal. Due to this incident coin tosses are now called before the coin is flipped, not while the coin is in the air.

1999 – Barry Sanders announces his retirement on July 27th. Groundbreaking for Ford Field takes place on November 16th. The Lions post a record of 8-8 and make the playoffs as a wild card.

2000 – The playoff game is held in Washington on January 8th and the Lions lose 13-27. During the 2000 season, Coach Bobby Ross resigns in November and is replaced by assistant Gary Moeller. The Lions go 9-7 but miss the playoffs when they fall to the Bears in the season finale.

2001 – The Lions last season at the Pontiac Silverdome. In January, the Lions appoint television football analyst and former NFL player Matt Millen as president and CEO. Millen fires Head Coach Gary Moeller and hires Marty Mornhinweg to replace him. The Lions go 2-14.

2002 – The Lions play their inaugural season at Ford Field. Their most memorable game of the year takes place November 24th in Champaign, Illinois. On a windy day, the Lions and Bears are tied at the end of regulation play. The Lions win the coin flip and, rather than choosing to receive the kickoff, decide to play with the wind at their backs. The Bears take the kickoff and drive down the field for the game-winning (into the wind) field goal. Mornhinweg is fired at the end of the season and leaves with a 5-27 record.

2003 – Matt Millen's procession of head coaches continues and his procession of wide receivers begins. Steve Mariucci is appointed head coach. The Lions use their first-round draft pick to select Michigan State University wide receiver Charles Rogers. The Lions finish the season 5-11.

2004 – The Lions select University of Texas wide receiver Roy Williams in the first round. Their season record is 6-10.

2005 – The Lions draft University of Southern California wide receiver Mike Williams in the first round. After four abysmal seasons of the Millen regime, Lions fans revolt. They wear paper bags over their heads, chant "Fire Millen!", display signs demanding his firing, and hold an angry-fan parade outside Ford Field. Following a Thanksgiving Day loss to the Falcons, coach Steve Mariucci is fired and replaced by Dick Jauron. The team posts a 5-11 record.

2006 – In January, the Lions fire Dick Jauron and hire Rod Marinelli. During the season the Lions compile a 3-13 record and the fan uprising continues: more paper bags, more chanting, more posters.

2007 – The Lions use their first-round pick to select Georgia Tech wide receiver Calvin Johnson. Fans are temporarily placated when the Lions start the season 6-2, but the team loses seven of the last eight games and finishes 7-9. It is the high-water mark of the Millen regime.

2008 – After the Lions lose their first three games, Matt Millen is fired. Millen leaves with a winning percentage of 27.7 percent. Fans celebrate, but then the unthinkable occurs: Lions lose the next thirteen games and post an 0-16 record. Head Coach Rod Marinelli is fired on December 29th. Martin Mayhew is named general manager.

2009 – Jim Schwartz is hired to coach the Lions. In March, defensive lineman Corey Smith dies in a boating accident off the Florida Gulf Coast. The Lions use the first pick in the NFL draft to select University of Georgia quarterback Matthew Stafford. The Lions go 2-14.

2010 – The Lions' 6-10 season is best remembered for the "Calvin Johnson Rule Game." On opening day in Chicago, the Lions trail by 5 points with 0:24 left in the game. Lions' quarterback Shaun Hill throws a pass to Calvin Johnson in the end zone. Johnson makes a brilliant catch and falls to the turf. With his knee already down, his hand holding the ball hits the ground and the ball pops out. The Lions think they won the game but the pass is ruled incomplete. This incident results in the NFL issuing the Calvin Johnson Rule which is a clarification of the existing rule that a receiver must maintain possession of the ball when he hits the ground.

2011 – Lions make the playoffs as a wild card with a 10-6 record.

2012 – In the playoff game on January 7th in New Orleans the Lions fall to the Saints 28-45. On Thanksgiving Day, the Lions are leading the Houston Texans in the third quarter when Texans' running back Justin Forsett is tackled for a 7-yard gain. Even though Forsett is clearly down, for some reason the referee doesn't blow the whistle and Forsett gets back up and runs to the end zone. Officials signal a touchdown. In a rage, Lions' Head Coach Jim Schwartz throws the challenge flag. But under NFL rules all touchdowns are automatically reviewed, and throwing a challenge flag in this situation is illegal. By throwing the challenge flag, Schwartz obligates the referee to cancel the automatic review and the "touchdown" stands. The Lions lose the game in overtime for their ninth Thanksgiving Day loss in a row. They finish the season 4-12.

2013 – The Lions go 7-9. Coach Jim Schwartz is fired in December.

2014 – In January, Jim Caldwell is hired to coach the Lions. On March 6th, William Clay Ford passes away at the age of 88. Control of the team passes to his wife Martha Firestone Ford. Lions go 11-5 and make the playoff as a wild card.

2015 – The playoff game is in Arlington, Texas on January 4th. The Lions jump to an early 14-0 lead, but the Cowboys mount a comeback and win 24-20. In the fourth quarter, a critical referee's call goes against the Lions when a defensive pass interference penalty against the Cowboys—*that the referee had announced*—is reversed. During the 2015 season, the Lions go 7-9 and the season's highlight is a victory over the Packers in Green Bay which is the Lions' first win there since 1991. However, the Packers turn the tables in the rematch in Detroit on December 3rd. With the Lions leading, the Packers attempt a desperation lateral play as time expires. The play is unsuccessful, but during the action a Lion defender hits Packers' quarterback Aaron Rogers's shoulder pad and an official mistakenly calls a facemask penalty. The Packers get one more play and use it to complete a Hail Mary that defeats the Lions 27-23. General Manager Martin Mayhew is fired; Sheldon White is named Interim GM.

2016 – On January 8th the Lions name Bob Quinn as general manager. Calvin Johnson retires in March. Lions make the playoffs as wild card with a 9-7 record.

2017 – In the playoff game in Seattle on January 7th, the Lions fall to the Seahawks 6-26. The Lions post another 9-7 record but miss the playoffs.

2018 – Jim Caldwell is fired on New Year's Day. Matt Patricia is hired to replace him. The Lions finish 6-10.

2019 – The Lions post a 3-12-1 record.

2020 – Martha Firestone Ford hands over control of the team to her daughter Sheila Ford Hamp. After the Lions lose 25-41 to the Houston Texans on Thanksgiving Day, Head Coach Matt Patricia and GM Bob Quinn are fired. Assistant Coach Darrell Bevell is appointed interim head coach. The Lions end the season 5-11.

2021 – In January, the Lions announce that Brad Holmes is general manager and Dan Campbell is head coach. Matthew Stafford is traded to the Los Angeles Rams for QB Jared Goff, two first-round picks, and a third-round pick. At Ford Field in the third game of the season, Baltimore Ravens' kicker Justin Tucker makes a record-setting 66-yard field goal as time expires to defeat the Lions 19-17. Two weeks later in Minneapolis, the Lions lose to the Vikings by the same score when kicker Greg Joseph hits a 54-yarder as time expires. The Lions become the only team in NFL history to lose twice in one season by last-second field goals longer than 50-yards. They end the season 3-13-1.

2022 – Lions' rebuilding program shows signs of success as the team posts a 9-8 record which includes 5-1 against divisional opponents. Detroit closes out the season by defeating the Packers in Green Bay.

DETROIT LIONS IN THE
PROFESSIONAL FOOTBALL HALL OF FAME

PLAYER	PRIMARY POSITION(S)	SEASONS WITH LIONS
Earl "Dutch" Clark	QB	1931-32, 1934-38
Alex Wojciechowicz	OL, LB	1938-46
Bill Dudley	DB, RB	1947-49
Lou Creekmur	OL	1950-59
Bobby Layne	QB	1950-58
Doak Walker	RB, K, P	1950-55
Jack Christiansen	DB	1951-58
Yale Lary	DB, P	1952-53, 1956-64
Dick Stanfel	OL	1952-55
Joe Schmidt	LB	1953-65
Frank Gatski	OL	1957
John Henry Johnson	RB	1957-59
Alex Karras	DL	1958-62, 1964-70
Dick LeBeau	DB	1959-72
Dick "Night Train" Lane	DB	1960-65
Ollie Matson	RB	1963
Hugh McElhenny	RB	1964
Lem Barney	DB	1967-77
Charlie Sanders	TE	1968-77
Curley Culp	DL	1980-81
Barry Sanders	RB	1989-98
Calvin "Megatron" Johnson	WR	2007-15

DETROIT LIONS' PLAYOFF APPEARANCES SINCE 1957

SEASON	RECORD	QUALIFIED AS	LOCATION	OUTCOME
1970	10-4	Wild Card	Dallas, TX	Cowboys 5, Lions 0
1982	4-5	8th Seed	Washington DC	Redskins 31, Lions 7
1983	9-7	Division Champ	San Francisco, CA	49ers 24, Lions 23
1991	12-4	Division Champ	Pontiac, MI	Lions 38, Cowboys 6
			Washington DC	Redskins 41, Lions 10
1993	10-6	Division Champ	Pontiac, MI	Packers 28, Lions 24
1994	9-7	Wild Card	Green Bay, WI	Packers 16, Lions 12
1995	10-6	Wild Card	Philadelphia, PA	Eagles 58, Lions 37
1997	9-7	Wild Card	Tampa, FL	Bucs 20, Lions 10
1999	8-8	Wild Card	Landover, MD	Redskins 27, Lions 13
2011	10-6	Wild Card	New Orleans, LA	Saints 45, Lions 28
2014	11-5	Wild Card	Arlington, TX	Cowboys 24, Lions 20
2016	9-7	Wild Card	Seattle, WA	Seahawks 26, Lions 6

The games listed here were played according to the format where a win advances the team toward the championship. The Playoff Bowls, which were staged during the 1960s between the two conference runners-up, are ignored because the winner did not advance beyond third place. The 1982 season was abbreviated due to a players' strike. Conference races were thrown out and at the end of the season the top eight teams in both conferences were seeded. The Lions were the #8 seed in the NFC, so they played #1 seed Washington.

Chapter 1
A Great Team Came and Went

There was a time when the Detroit Lions were the top franchise in the National Football League. That may be hard for modern-day Lions fans to believe, but it's true. It happened during the 1950s when over a six-year span the Lions played in four NFL Championship Games and won three of them.[1] The Lions teams of that era were so deep in talent that nine of their players are enshrined in the Professional Football Hall of Fame in Canton, Ohio.

The franchise began as the Portsmouth (Ohio) Spartans. They joined the NFL in 1930, and four years later were bought by a Detroit area businessman named George Richards. He moved the team to Detroit, and changed its name to Lions. The franchise had several quality players including Ernie Caddel, quarterback Earl "Dutch" Clark (HOF), and player/coach George "Potsy" Clark.[2] The Lions enjoyed quick success in Detroit, placing second in the Western Conference in 1934. Then, in 1935, the Lions won the West and met the Eastern Conference champion New York Giants in the NFL Championship Game. The Lions won 26-7 and claimed their first NFL title.

Success, however, didn't last. The Lions soon fell to middle-of-the-pack in the standings, then hit bottom during the 1940s. In 1942, their record was 0-11; it was a horrid season when the Lions scored 38 points, gave up 238 points, and were shutout five times. In fact, the 1940s were so dismal that the team acquired a reputation as the "NFL's Appalachia" and a "graveyard for coaches."[3]

Seeds of change were sown in 1948 when an ownership group headed by D. Lyle Fife and Edwin Anderson purchased the team.[4] One of their first moves was to hire Indiana University's Bo McMillin as head coach, and he began assembling the group that would dominate the NFL during the 1950s. McMillin acquired, among others, Les Bingaman, Cloyce Box, Lou Creekmer (HOF), Leon Hart, Bob Hoernschemeyer, Bobby Layne (HOF), Bob Smith, and Doak Walker (HOF).[5] In 1950, the team posted a 6-6 record—their best in years—but the players didn't think McMillin could take them to the championship. So, with the players' support, the Lions' owners bought out McMillin's contract and promoted Assistant Coach Buddy Parker to lead the team. Parker was a wheeler-dealer who—along with General Manager Nick Kerbawy—traded and drafted the Lions to eventual prosperity.[6] In 1951, the team's additions included Jack Christensen (HOF), Pat Harder, and Jim Martin. The Lions went 7-4-1 which was good for second place in the conference, a half game behind the 8-4 Los Angeles Rams. In fact, the Lions were five minutes away from winning the conference because that's how much time was left in the final game of the season at San Francisco when the Lions led 17-14. But a late 49ers' touchdown knocked Detroit out of the Championship Game. The Lions were close to the top, but not quite there.

Three Championships in Six Years

Reaching the summit wasn't easy. The Lions added Yale Lary (HOF) and Dick Stanfel (HOF) in 1952, but began the season 1-2 with both losses coming at the hands of the San Francisco 49ers by a combined score of 45-3. Then the team caught fire, winning eight of their next nine games to finish the season 9-3 and tied with the LA Rams for first-place in the Western Conference. The teams met in a playoff game at Briggs Stadium on December 21st.[7] The Lions outplayed the Rams through the first three quarters for a 24-7 lead, but then the Rams scored 14 points to narrow the margin to 24-21. With less than a minute remaining, the Lions sealed the victory by intercepting a pass deep in the Rams' end, and moments later scored a touchdown for a 31-21 victory. The Championship Game was held a week later in Cleveland, and the Lions' defense was outstanding that day, holding the Browns to just 7 points. The Lions won their second NFL Championship with a 17-7 victory.

The team was strengthened in 1953 with the additions of rookies Charlie Ane and Joe Schmidt (HOF). They won the Western Conference with a 10-2 record, then once again faced Cleveland in the Championship Game, this time in Detroit. The Lions led 10-3 at halftime, but Cleveland scored 13 points in the second half to take a 16-10 lead with just over four minutes left in the game. The Lions then drove 80 yards for the tying touchdown, and the extra point was the margin of victory. The Lions had a 17-16 victory and their third NFL Championship.[8]

The 1954 Lions won the Western Conference and, for the third straight year, met the Browns in the NFL Championship Game. This game had a different outcome. Playing in Cleveland, the Lions jumped to an early 3-0 lead but then things fell apart. Nine turnovers by the Lions (three fumbles, six interceptions) and penalties at key moments doomed their effort. Cleveland took revenge with a 56-10 victory.

The next season, a combination of retirements (including Les Bingaman and Cloyce Box) and injuries pushed the Lions from first to last place. Bobby Layne hurt his arm while handling a horse during the offseason and then injured his knee during the season. He was never right that year, and the Lions brought in Harry Gilmer to back him up. Detroit ended the season 3-9.

The team bounced back in 1956. Layne was healthy again, and while they lost Bob Hoernschemeyer and Doak Walker to retirement, they gained back the services of several players who'd been serving military obligations, including Yale Lary.[9] After winning their first six games there was talk of an undefeated season. But the Lions lost two of the next five and entered the season finale a half-game behind their opponents the Chicago Bears. A victory would put the Lions in the Championship Game.

The game didn't go the Lions' way. In the first half, Chicago linebacker Ed Meadows knocked Bobby Layne out of the game on what the Lions thought was a late hit. After pitching the ball to running back Gene Gedman, Layne was blindsided by Meadows.[10] Layne suffered a concussion and was taken to a hospital. Meadows wasn't penalized, but was ejected later in the half for a foul against running back Bill Bowman. The Lions lost 21-38 and their season was over.

As the 1957 season approached it was unclear how the team would fare. Bobby Layne—a notorious partier—was 30 years old and past his prime. To back up Layne, Coach Buddy Parker signed Green Bay quarterback Tobin Rote which turned out to be a brilliant move. Parker also acquired longtime Cleveland Browns' center Frank Gatski (HOF), San Francisco star running back John Henry Johnson (HOF), and drafted defensive back Terry Barr and lineman John Gordy. Then, after making these moves that were instrumental in helping the Lions secure another championship, Parker pulled one of the biggest surprises in Lions' history: he resigned.

Ongoing issues between Parker and the Lions' owners came to a head on the evening of August 12, 1957, at the annual Meet the Lions banquet. One source of friction was the duration of Parker's contracts. Parker had been working on one-year contracts, all the while seeking longer-term deals.[11] The owners finally relented and in 1957 signed him to a two-year contract, but Parker's resentment lingered. He was also bothered about the owners increasingly palling around with the players, something Parker "detested."[12] When Parker walked into a pre-banquet party and saw the owners and players drinking together, he left in a rage. Parker attended the banquet and when introduced to the crowd stepped up to the microphone and announced that he was quitting. There was stunned silence, but he wasn't joking. Buddy Parker, the primary architect of the Lions' 1950s dynasty, had quit.[13]

The Lions promoted Assistant Coach George Wilson to head coach. The season didn't start well; after six games the Lions were 3-3, but at least the West Coast trip was over (it resulted in two losses). Wilson had quarterbacks Layne and Rote splitting time, the coach playing whomever he thought had the hotter hand. The team caught fire and went on a 5-1 run, but not without hitting a bump along the way. Against the Browns on December 8th at Briggs Stadium, Bobby Layne suffered a broken leg and dislocated ankle. Fortunately, thanks to Buddy Parker, Tobin Rote was on the team. Rote took over full-time quarterback duties and the Lions finished 8-4 and tied with San Francisco for first place in the West.

The playoff game took place in San Francisco on December 22nd. The 49ers came out strong and ran up a 24-7 halftime lead. The Lions' players later said the walls in the locker room were so thin that during halftime they could hear the 49ers talking about how they were going to spend their playoff bonuses. This infuriated the Lions and they played solid football in the second half, taking a 28-27 lead early in the fourth quarter. San Francisco was held scoreless the rest of the way, and the Lions won 31-27 which advanced them to the NFL Championship Game.

Their opponents in the title game were, yet again, the Cleveland Browns. This game was played in Detroit on December 29th and the Lions avenged the humiliating 1954 loss by crushing Cleveland 59-14. The Lions had won their third NFL Championship since 1952, and their fourth overall.

Three NFL Championships in six years for the Detroit Lions. Can you imagine?

Into the Desert

The Lions haven't played in a title game since 1957. They've come close a few times: quality teams in 1962, 1970, 1983, and 1991 might've won championships if some breaks had gone their way (these near-misses are the subject of the next chapter). But if we set aside those four seasons, Lions fans have lived in a desert that has gone on for over six decades. Yes, there have been thirteen playoff games, but only once did the Lions win and advance. Instead of success, Lions' fans have mostly watched sixty-plus years of futility: untimely fumbles; interceptions; missed tackles; blown pass coverages; missed field goals; penalties; losing. During some seasons the team was hapless, serving as props while their opponents created highlight reels.

The numbers tell the story. From 1958-2022, the Lions' record in regular season and playoff games is 417 wins, 572 losses, and 19 ties, or a win rate of 42 percent.[14] By contrast, the Minnesota Vikings, the Lions' most successful divisional rival (in terms of winning the division), have won 54 percent of their games since they began as an expansion team in 1961.[15] During their life as an NFL franchise, the Vikings have won over 100 more games than the Lions (over the same time period), and it has resulted in a huge difference in divisional titles by the two teams. Both teams became part of the NFL's Central Division when it was formed in 1967 (the name was changed to NFC North in 2002), and here are the number of titles won by teams in the division:

NFC CENTRAL/NORTH DIVISION TITLES, 1967-2022

Minnesota Vikings	21
Green Bay Packers	18
Chicago Bears	11
Detroit Lions	3
Tampa Bay Buccaneers (1977-2001)	3

Over fifty-four seasons the Vikings won 37 percent of the division titles while the Lions won 5 percent. It's a stunning difference. The paucity of Lions' division titles helps explain their record in playoff games. Lions fans know their team has done badly since 1957, the playoff record since the last championship is 1-12.[16] One of the reasons why is that since the Lions have rarely been divisional champs, they've rarely hosted playoff games. In fact, in those thirteen playoff games they've had home field advantage just twice: for a divisional round game during the 1991 season, and as division champs hosting a wild card in 1993.[17] In the 1991 game they scored a smashing victory, and in 1993 they lost to a quality opponent on a blown pass coverage late in the fourth quarter. The other eleven playoff games were on the road and the Lions lost all of them.

An Unusual Franchise

The Detroit Lions occupy an unusual place in the professional sports world. They've been in a league for over ninety years, won an early championship, suffered a drought, became a powerful dynasty, and then went over sixty years without reaching another championship game. How many other North American professional sports teams fit that general description?

Not many. The Cleveland Browns are the only other "old" NFL team to have never played in a Super Bowl. This is ironic because they were the Lions' chief rival during the 1950s. The Browns won four NFL Championships from 1950-1964, and since then have lost a Championship Game (1965), and on five occasions have been one victory away from the Super Bowl.

The Chicago Cubs were baseball's version of the Lions before winning the World Series in 2016. The Cubs were a successful franchise during the first half of the Twentieth Century, appearing in nine World Series from 1906-1938, and then reaching the Series again in 1945. After that, they were famous also-rans, going over seventy years before being crowned champions in 2016. When the Cubs won it all that year, Lions' fans took note: maybe there *is* hope.

In ice hockey, the Toronto Maple Leafs have had a similar experience to the Lions. The Maple Leafs last drank champagne from the Stanley Cup in 1967, and it came at the end of a great run: it was the Leafs' fourth Stanley Cup in six years. Few Toronto fans in 1967 could have imagined their team's bleak future.

A few National Basketball Association teams have been remarkably unsuccessful. The Sacramento Kings last won a championship in 1951 as the Rochester (NY) Royals. The Atlanta Hawks last appearance in the NBA Finals was in 1961 as the St. Louis Hawks. The Los Angeles Clippers have been around since 1970 and never been to the NBA Finals.

Meanwhile, a handful of sports franchises have won multiple championships over many years. The New York Yankees are the most successful major league franchise in North America. Over the last 100 years, the Yankees have appeared in 40 percent of the World Series and won 27 percent of them. The NFL's New England Patriots, created in 1960 as part of the American Football League (AFL), have won 57 percent of their games. Since 1985, the team has appeared in eleven Super Bowls and won six. Over the last forty years, the NBA's Los Angeles Lakers have been to the finals nineteen times and won eleven championships.

Then there are rare teams that accomplished great things early in their lives. In 2018, the NHL's Las Vegas Golden Knights played in the Stanley Cup Finals *in their first season of existence*. The 1995 NFL's Carolina Panthers and Jacksonville Jaguars were one game from the Super Bowl in their second year of existence.

Questions arise. Why is it that the New England Patriots have appeared in eleven Super Bowls and the Detroit Lions in none? Why do the Minnesota Vikings have twenty-one NFC Central/North Division titles and the Lions just three? How could the Carolina Panthers and Jacksonville Jaguars accomplish something in their second year of existence that the Lions have managed just once in over half a century?

Management is the Key

There's an old saying about organizations: success starts at the top. Over time, an organization's success depends on the quality of its management. In a sports franchise, management selects coaches and players. Management decides when to stick with the status quo and when to make changes. Management quality distinguishes successful sports franchises from unsuccessful sports franchises. The New England Patriots have been more successful than the Detroit Lions because they've had superior players and coaches. Where did those players and coaches come from? They were selected by management. In other words, the Patriots have been a better managed team than the Lions.

Back in the 1950s, good management was responsible for the Lions' dynasty. Owners Anderson and Fife hired Bo McMillin as head coach and he acquired players who contributed mightily to the championship teams of a few years later. When the players told the owners that McMillin wasn't the man who could lead them to the championship, the owners bought out McMillin's contract and put Buddy Parker in charge. The owners then got out of the way and let Parker and General Manager Kerbawy assemble the talent that Parker coached to success. Eventually Anderson and Fife had a falling out, and Parker grew unhappy and left the team.[18] But the dynasty had one more great season left because there was inertia and George Wilson was a quality coach. The Lions won the championship in 1957, went into decline, but then were able to reload into contenders again by the early 1960s. In fact, of all the Lions' teams since 1957, the one that came closest to reaching a championship game was the 1962 version.

Shortly after the 1962 near-miss, a management change took place that altered the course of the Detroit Lions. In 1963, William Clay ("Bill") Ford (who had become a part-owner in 1961) negotiated a deal to buy out the other team owners. He took formal control in January 1964, and the Ford family has owned the Lions ever since. Bill Ford ran the team until he died in 2014, control then passed to his wife Martha Firestone Ford. In 2020 she handed it off to daughter Shelia Ford Hamp. Since 1964 the Detroit Lions have had nine general managers, over twenty head coaches, scores of assistant coaches, over a thousand players, and one family in control. An observer is left to conclude that the root cause of the Detroit Lions' lack of on-field success has been the Ford family's poor management of the team.

This mismanagement has manifested as frequent coaching changes, a string of head coaches who (with one exception) never again served as head coaches in the NFL, and general managers—Russ Thomas and Matt Millen in particular—who failed to produce winning teams yet retained their jobs for years. Lions' fans have watched a parade of coaches and players pass through the organization and generate results which, except for a few seasons, have been remarkably devoid of success.

Some Great Players

One aspect that has confused Lions' fans over the years is how their team has had so little on-field success while employing some truly great players. Alex Karras (HOF), Dick Lane (HOF), Yale Lary (HOF), Dick LeBeau (HOF), Joe Schmidt (HOF), and Wayne Walker were among the NFL's best defensive players of the 1960s. In the late 1960s and into the 1970s, Lem Barney (HOF), Mel Farr, Ed Flanagan, Steve Owens, and Charlie Sanders (HOF) were at the top of the game. Then came the "Silver Rush" defensive linemen Al Baker, Doug English, William Gay, Dave Pureifory, and John Woodcock, and they were joined by running back Billy Sims in 1980. Jerry Ball, Bennie Blades, Lomas Brown, Kevin Glover, Herman Moore, and Chris Spielman came later. Barry Sanders (HOF)—who some consider the greatest running back to ever set foot on a gridiron—played for the team from 1989-1998. In more recent times the Lions enjoyed the play of Calvin Johnson (HOF) and Ndamukong Suh. Matthew Stafford was the Lions' best quarterback since Bobby Layne and will likely end up in the Hall of Fame.

How could a team have so many great players and never reach the Super Bowl?

The answer, of course, is that a few stars do not make a football team. It takes eleven offensive starters, eleven defensive starters, and assorted special teams players and backups to field a football team. Having a Barry Sanders isn't enough. It takes many great players to win championships, and this seems to be where the Lions have come up short. Management has found occasional superstars, but not enough additional talent to reach the top. Bill Walsh, the coach responsible for the San Francisco dynasty of the 1980s, once said, "Championships are won with the bottom half of the roster."[19] Perhaps this is where the Lions have come up short.

Problem Opponents

Another odd feature of the Lions has been their tendency to be owned by other teams. The Minnesota Vikings were a huge thorn in the Lions' side from the late 1960s until the early 1980s, and then again in the 2000s. During the darkest years, from 1968-1979, the Lions record against the Vikings was 3-21. The Detroit media called it a hex and, whatever it was, caused the Lions and their fans an enormous amount of grief because there were seasons when the Lions had solid teams but couldn't win their division because they couldn't beat the Vikings.

The Green Bay Packers played this role from the 1990s-2010s. During the worst stretch from November 1992 - October 2013, the Lions and Packers met forty-five times and the Lions record in those games was 10-35. At home they were 10-12, which means the road record was 0-23. Yes, it's true: over a twenty-two year span the Detroit Lions lost every game they played in Green Bay.[20]

The Washington Commanders, formerly known as the Braves, Redskins, and Washington Football Team, are another franchise that has caused much pain to the Lions and their fans. There have been seasons when Washington was a hurdle between the Lions and the Super Bowl that the Lions couldn't jump (in 1991 Washington was the final hurdle). An incredible fact is that the Detroit Lions never won a game in Washington DC, and they tried for over sixty years.

The Move Indoors

In the early 1970s, Lions' owner Bill Ford made a management decision that seemed like a good idea at the time, but appears to have contributed to the Lions' lack of on-field success. This was the decision to commit the Lions to play their home games at an indoor stadium to be built by the City of Pontiac, Michigan. The deal was signed in 1971, and construction of the stadium began shortly thereafter. The Lions played their last home game at Tiger Stadium on Thanksgiving Day, 1974, and then in 1975 began play at the Pontiac Silverdome. Thus, the Lions went from being an outdoor team to an indoor team.

They've remained indoors ever since. The Silverdome eventually became economically obsolete so the team bought out their lease and partnered with the City of Detroit to build Ford Field which is another covered stadium. The Lions played their final season at the Silverdome in 2001, and moved to Ford Field in 2002.

The original motivation for moving the team indoors was a combination of profit and concern for fan comfort. Tiger Stadium had problems as a football venue—bad sight lines and a capacity of around 53,000. Also, fans were exposed to the elements, and winters back then were colder than in recent years. Ford wanted a larger, better stadium—with a roof if possible—for the team's financial bottom-line and fan comfort.

The reasoning behind the move was sound. However, at the time no one realized that indoor teams would be less successful than outdoor teams in terms of reaching and winning Super Bowls. Nobody knew because there was almost no data; in the early 1970s the Houston Oilers were the only indoor NFL team, and they'd been playing in the Houston Astrodome for just a few years.

Chapter 6 describes some of the problems faced by indoor teams, and offers explanations for why they have reached far fewer Super Bowls than outdoor teams. Playing indoors isn't the only reason for the Lions lack of success, but it is surely one of them.

A Season for the Ages

In 2008, the Detroit Lions made history for the wrong reason. That was the season they became the first team to finish a regular season with an 0-16 record. The record was matched nine years later by the Lions' 1950s rivals, the Cleveland Browns.

The NFL's sixteen-game season was in effect from 1978-2020. This means that for forty-three seasons about thirty teams played sixteen games a year. That's over a thousand team-seasons, and only the Detroit Lions (2008) and Cleveland Browns (2017) managed to do it without posting a win. Accomplishing this feat required a rare combination of incompetence and bad luck. In the Lions' case it was the final sad act of the Matt Millen Era, a dark time in Detroit football history named after the man who was president and general manager of the Lions for eight long years. His legacy is discussed in chapters 7 and 8. The NFL moved to the seventeen-game season in 2021, so football fans wonder: will a team surpass the Lions and Browns by going 0-17?

Since the winless season the Lions have lived in a sea of mediocrity except for a few seasons—most notably 2014—when they reached the playoffs but were unable to advance.

During this time the coaching parade continued: four head coaches passed through the door in thirteen years.

Lions' Lore and Moving Forward

The Lions have experienced many adventures since 1957, some happy, some tragic, and some best described as bizarre. Some of the notables are described in Chapter 11. The book concludes with thoughts on strategies as the Lions move forward. Can the Lions end their losing ways?

We begin the Lions' post-1957 odyssey by examining the four Lions teams that came closest to reaching NFL title games. Had a few breaks gone their way, it might've happened.

SOME NOTABLE LIONS OF THE 1952-57 DYNASTY ERA

PLAYER	PRIMARY POSITION(S)	SEASONS WITH LIONS	NUMBER OF CHAMPIONSHIPS	HOF?
Les Bingaman	DL	1948-54	2	
Cloyce Box	WR, RB	1949-50, 1952-54	2	
Bob Smith	DB, P	1949-54	2	
Lou Creekmur	OL	1950-59	3	Yes
Leon Hart	WR, RB	1950-57	3	
Bob Hoernschemeyer	RB	1950-55	2	
Bobby Layne	QB	1950-58	3	Yes
Doak Walker	RB, K, P	1950-55	2	Yes
Jack Christiansen	DB	1951-58	3	Yes
Pat Harder	RB	1951-53	2	
Jim Martin	OL, LB, K	1951-61	3	
Yale Lary	DB, P	1952-53, 1956-64	3	Yes
Dick Stenfel	OL	1952-55	2	Yes
Joe Schmidt	LB	1953-65	2	Yes
Terry Barr	DB, RB, WR	1957-65	1	
Frank Gatski	OL	1957	1	Yes
John Gordy	OL	1957-67	1	
John Henry Johnson	RB	1957-59	1	Yes
Tobin Rote	QB	1957-59	1	

This list should not be considered exhaustive.
HOF = member of the Professional Football Hall of Fame.

Chapter 2
Four Times They Came Close

Since 1957, the Detroit Lions have been through sixty-plus seasons with varying degrees of success. There have been no championship game appearances, but they reached the playoffs thirteen times. So, in theory there have been thirteen seasons when the Lions passed the first hurdle on the path to the ultimate game. In reality, however, the odds of many of those Lions' playoff teams reaching the Super Bowl were extremely small. For example, no one expected the 1982 Lions with their 4-5 record during the strike-shortened season to advance in the playoffs, especially since they were matched up in the first round against #1 seed Washington. Nor did anyone expect the 1999 Detroit Lions with their 8-8 record to go far. The majority of Lions' playoff teams were bubble teams that qualified as wild cards. While wild cards do occasionally reach (and win) Super Bowls, it is rare (about 5 percent of wild cards have reached the ultimate game). It has usually been a team on a hot streak at the end of the season.

That description fits a few Lions' wild card teams, in particular the 1970 and 1995 editions. The 1970 team ended the season on a five-game winning streak, had four future Hall of Famers on the roster, and were favored in their playoff game against Dallas (described later in this chapter). The 1995 team was a similar story: they looked to be going nowhere at midseason, then won their final seven games—which included rousing come-from-behind victories—and made the playoffs. They, too, were favored in their playoff game, this one against the Eagles in Philadelphia.

Unfortunately, the Lions laid an egg in the City of Brotherly Love. The first quarter ended in a 7-7 tie, then the bottom fell out. Pretty much anything you can imagine going wrong for a football team happened to the Lions in the second quarter. Turnovers, penalties, missed tackles, missed blocks, a short punt. The Eagles scored 31 unanswered points, and the misery continued into the third quarter. At one point, the Lions were behind 7-51. They mounted a bit of a comeback, but the final score was 58-37. Seven Lions' turnovers led to four Philadelphia touchdowns and two field goals. The game was an utter disaster.

Another wild card team that stood out was the 2014 Lions. This is the team that suffered the painful playoff loss in Dallas, the game where the Lions jumped out to a 14-0 first quarter lead, were ahead 20-7 in the third quarter, and then watched their lead shrink and finally disappear as the Cowboys won 24-20. With the game on the line in the fourth quarter, the Lions fumbled twice and shanked a punt. What is better remembered is the pass interference call/no call against Dallas. The obvious penalty, which would have extended a Lions' drive, was announced and then—incredibly and inexplicably—cancelled (this incident is described in Chapter 10). The officials' blunder may have cost the Lions the game. If the Lions had won, would they have advanced further in the playoffs? It wasn't likely because Detroit was the NFC's #6 seed, so their next game would have been at #1 seed Seattle. But you never know.

Since 1957, the Lions have won three division titles—in 1983, 1991, and 1993. Of the three, the 1993 team was probably the least likely to reach the Super Bowl. They were 7-2 after nine games, and then went 3-4 to finish the season 10-6. NFL fans know how important it is for a team to be playing their best football at the end of the season, not at the start. After closing out the regular season by beating the Packers 30-20 at the Silverdome, the Lions met them again a week later in the playoffs (the Packers were wild cards). Conventional wisdom in the NFL says it's difficult to beat the same team twice in consecutive games, especially if the teams are closely matched (which was true of the Lions and Packers that year). The game was at the Silverdome, and the Lions had a 24-21 lead with a minute remaining when Packers' quarterback Brett Favre extended a play by moving out of the pocket. Meanwhile, receiver Sterling Sharpe ran into the back right-corner of the end zone with the nearest defender yards away. Readers who don't know what happened next can guess. The Lions lost 24-28. Had the Lions won they would've traveled to San Francisco to play the 49ers who had destroyed them by a score of 55-17 on December 19th at the Silverdome.

The 1983 and 1991 Lions had better shots at reaching the Super Bowl. But before we discuss those teams, let's look at two other contenders.

1962: One Bad Play

Of all the Lions' teams since 1957, the 1962 version might've had the best chance of winning a championship. But their season was doomed by one bad play late in the fourth quarter of an early-season game.

The Lions' fortunes had declined after the 1957 Championship. Age caught up with the team, and they fell to 4-7-1 in 1958, and then 3-8-1 in 1959. Meanwhile, they were acquiring new talent through drafts and trades, and began to show improvement in the early 1960s. The 1960 Lions went 7-5, and in 1961 their record was 8-5-1. They finished both seasons in second place in the Western Conference.

At the start of the 1962 season only five players were left from the 1957 champions: offensive linemen John Gordy and Harley Sewell, defensive lineman Darris McCord, linebacker Joe Schmidt (HOF), and defensive back Yale Lary (HOF). The rest of the 1957 roster had retired or been traded, and their replacements included star players such as defensive backs Dick Lane (HOF) and Dick LeBeau (HOF), linebacker Wayne Walker, and defensive linemen Roger Brown and Alex Karris (HOF). Thus, the 1962 Lions had five future Hall of Famers on defense. On offense, there was a solid line, Ollie Matson and Tom Watkins at running back, wide receivers Gail Cogdill and Terry Barr, and tight end John Gibbons. It was a talented team.

One problem facing the Lions since 1957 had been the quarterback position. When the 1958 season began, Bobby Layne, who had been badly injured in 1957, was past his prime and unhappy about splitting time with Tobin Rote. Meanwhile, Buddy Parker had landed the head coaching job in Pittsburgh and wanted Layne on his team. A trade was negotiated sending Layne to the Steelers in exchange for quarterback Earl Morrall and two draft picks. This is when the supposed Curse of Bobby Layne was born. The urban legend (which has never been substantiated) is that upon learning of the trade, Layne announced that the Lions wouldn't win another championship for fifty years.

The losing seasons of 1958 and 1959 put Tobin Rote out of favor. Coach George Wilson wanted a better arm, so Rote was released after the 1959 season. In early 1960, the Lions acquired quarterback Jim Ninowski from Cleveland; he and Morrall were the Lions' quarterbacks heading into the 1960s. However, Ninowski didn't work out as well as Coach Wilson had hoped, so he was shipped back to Cleveland in 1962 as part of a six-player trade. Among the players the Lions received were quarterback Milt Plum and running back Tom Watkins. Plum had been the NFL's leading passer during 1960 and 1961 and was viewed as the solution to the Lions' quarterback problem. Heading into the 1962 season, the plan was for Plum to start and Morrall to serve as backup.[21]

The reigning NFL Champion Green Bay Packers were considered the team to beat. Head Coach Vince Lombardi had arrived in Green Bay in 1959, and two years later won the first of his five NFL Championships.[22] The 1961 Packers demolished the opposition, winning the West with an 11-3 record (the Lions were second at 8-5-1), and then shutting out the New York Giants 37-0 in the NFL Championship game. If the Lions were going to do anything big in 1962, they had to win the West and that meant beating the Packers at least once, preferably twice.

The season started out well for Detroit. Opening day brought Buddy Parker, Bobby Layne, and the rest of the Pittsburgh Steelers to Tiger Stadium. The Lions won handily 45-7. The next week they beat the 49ers in Detroit, then went on the road to Baltimore and scored another victory. The Lions were 3-0, tied with Green Bay for first place, and it looked like Plum was the quarterback they'd been seeking. The next game was enormous: it pitted the Lions against the Packers in Green Bay, and the winner would have a one-game lead in the conference. The Lions headed to Wisconsin believing they were the better team.[23]

The game was a defensive struggle played on a wet, muddy field. On their first possession, the Packers drove into the Detroit end and were stopped at the 7-yard line. They settled for a field goal. Detroit scored their lone touchdown in the second quarter. The sequence began when Joe Schmidt blitzed and forced a fumble by Packers' quarterback Bart Starr. Alex Karras recovered the ball on the Green Bay 34. The Lions' offense moved the ball down to the 6, then scored when running back Danny Lewis turned the corner and ran into the end zone. The extra point made it 7-3.

The only scoring in the third quarter was a Green Bay field goal, so when the fourth quarter began the Lions were ahead 7-6. Both teams missed long field goal attempts, the Packers' coming with about six minutes left. Their 47-yard try came up short and was returned by the Lions to their own 22-yard line. With the lead and the ball, the Lions moved the line of scrimmage out to their own 49 and took about five minutes off the clock doing so. With 1:06 remaining the Lions faced third down. Green Bay had one timeout left; if the Lions could convert the first down the game would effectively be over.

With the clock stopped on a timeout, George Wilson, quarterback Milt Plum, and receiver Terry Barr met on the sideline. After talking on the phone to an assistant in the press box, Wilson made his decision: pass the ball. He left it up to Plum which pass-play to call.

According to some reports, Joe Schmidt told Milt Plum to call a running play. The idea was that if the Lions came up short of the first down, then Green Bay would be forced to burn their final timeout. Detroit could rely on Yale Lary, one of the best punters in the NFL, to pin the Packers deep in their own end. Green Bay would be forced to move down the field with about a minute left on the clock.

Plum went back to the huddle and called the 8 and 5, slant in, slant out play. Wide receivers Gail Cogdill and Terry Barr, lined up on opposite sides, would both start forward, then slant toward the middle, then cut again and slant toward the corners. Slant in, slant out. Plum would throw to one of them on the slant out. The play had been used twice in the game on third downs and worked both times.

The third time wasn't the charm. A slant pass is a timing play where the quarterback throws the ball to a spot where the receiver is supposed to be. Terry Barr was the chosen target, and he slanted in, but the trouble occurred when he made his cut to slant out. He slipped in the mud. Plum threw the ball to where Barr was supposed to be, but he wasn't there. Instead, Packers' cornerback Herb Adderly (HOF) had fallen back in coverage and was in position to take the throw. Adderly intercepted on the Packers' 40 and returned the ball to the Lions' 18.

Two Packers' running plays advanced the ball to the 14, and then Paul Horning (HOF) kicked a field goal with 0:27 left. The Packers had a 9-7 lead, and Detroit was unable to stage a miracle at the end. The final gun sounded and the Lions left the field stunned losers; defeat had been stolen from the jaws of victory.

In the locker room, all hell broke loose. There are varying stories about what happened, but we know that Alex Karras threw his helmet at Milt Plum and missed by about two inches.[24] There are reports that other players, including Joe Schmidt, went after Plum although Schmidt said he didn't do it. According to Detroit sportswriter Jerry Green, Plum had to be rescued by Head Coach George Wilson. Many of the players thought Plum had called the pass play (which he had, although Wilson told him to pass). Afterwards, Wilson accepted responsibility.[25] Plum later said, "George called for a pass. But I called the pattern. Maybe I shouldn't have listened to him. Something inside me told me we should have been running."[26]

The failed pass-play likely cost the Lions the game and, quite possibly, the NFL Championship. Green Bay lost only one game that season: the rematch in Detroit on Thanksgiving Day. Considered one of the Lions' greatest wins since 1957, the team played inspired football and thoroughly outplayed the Packers at Tiger Stadium. The score was 26-0 at the end of the third quarter, and the Lions ultimately prevailed 26-14.

The Lions finished the season 11-3. Their three losses were to the Packers, Giants, and the final game to the Bears by a score of 3-0. The last game was a meaningless exercise for the Lions because the Packers had won the West and were advancing to the Championship Game. The outcome of the Lions/Bears' game might have been different had it mattered.

If the Lions had won that game in Green Bay, they would have finished the season 12-2 and tied for first place with the Packers. A playoff game would have been held to determine which team advanced to the Championship Game. If the Lions had also beaten the Bears in the season finale, they would have been 13-1 and gone straight to the Championship Game.

As things turned out, the Packers met the New York Giants for the championship. The final score was Packers 16, Giants 7, and Vince Lombardi had the second of his five NFL Championships. The Detroit Lions were relegated to the Playoff Bowl (aka the Runner-Up Bowl) where they defeated the Pittsburgh Steelers 17-10.

The 1962 season was a missed opportunity that many consider the Lions' closest brush with a Championship since 1957. Several players on that team spent the rest of their lives believing the Lions were better than the Packers that year.

1970: Shutout in Dallas

Detroit Lions' legend Joe Schmidt was a linebacker and defensive play-caller known for his speed, tackling ability, and football smarts. Considered one of the NFL's greatest defensive players of all-time, he was a ten-season first-team Pro Bowler, named to the NFL's All-Decade Team for the 1950s, and inducted into the Professional Football Hall of Fame in 1973. The Lions have honored Schmidt by retiring his jersey's #56.

After hanging up his cleats at the conclusion of the 1965 season, Schmidt was hired by the Lions to be assistant linebackers' coach. The team was in decline at the time and posted a 4-9-1 record in 1966. Owner William Clay Ford fired Head Coach Harry Gilmer (who'd replaced George Wilson in 1965) and elevated Schmidt to the position. Schmidt, a few days shy of his thirty-fifth birthday, signed a five-year contract. Charged with rebuilding the team, he would work alongside new General Manager Russ Thomas.[27] Schmidt was in charge of draft choices and trades while Thomas was responsible for signing players to contracts.

The rebuilding program got off to a great start as the 1967 draft was perhaps the Lions' best ever. They selected Lem Barney (HOF), Mel Farr, Paul Naumoff, and Mike Weger. Barney was a cornerback with a knack for intercepting passes and kick returner extraordinaire. Mel Farr was a running back with blazing speed and quickness who was also an accomplished receiver. Naumoff was a linebacker who missed only two games during his twelve seasons with the Lions. Weger, another defensive stalwart, was a safety who played nine seasons for the Lions. In one draft the Lions bagged four long-term starters, one of whom ended up in the Hall of Fame. At the end of the 1967 season, Farr was named NFL's Offensive Rookie of the Year, and Barney was Defensive Rookie of the Year.

Schmidt told fans the rebuilding program would take time and on-cue the team stumbled out of the gate. Their first preseason game was against the Broncos in Denver, and it was the first-ever contest between teams from the NFL and AFL (this was three years before the merger). Supremely confident, Alex Karras said he'd walk home from Denver if the Lions lost. The Lions did lose, by a score of 7-13, but Karras didn't make good on his promise. He took the team flight back to Detroit.

The team scored again in the 1968 draft. They used their first-round pick on University of Massachusetts quarterback Greg Landry, and then chose wide receiver Earl McCullough, a world-class sprinter and hurdler from USC.[28] In the third round they took a tight end from the University of Minnesota named Charlie Sanders (HOF). Landry would spend years as the Lions starting quarterback, McCullough was the 1968 NFL Offensive Rookie of the Year and a Lion for six years, and Sanders—a brilliant receiver and punishing blocker—went on to become one of the greatest tight ends in NFL history.

It took a while for the draft picks to influence the team's win-loss record. The 1968 team was 4-8-2. The following spring they had had another quality draft, choosing running back Altie Taylor, receiver Larry Walton, and offensive linemen Jim Yarbrough and Rocky Rasley. The rebuilding effort bore fruit: the 1969 team went 9-4-1 but came in second in the division behind the Minnesota Vikings.

The 1970 draft wasn't as productive as the previous three. Part of the problem was the Lions' improved record in 1969 meant that they were selecting from further down the list. But they did get Heisman Trophy winner Steve Owens. Owens was a running back from the University of Oklahoma and a big part of the Lions' offense until he suffered a career-ending knee injury in the Lions' last-ever game at Tiger Stadium in 1974. They also drafted defensive lineman Jim Mitchell and punter Herman "Thunderfoot" Weaver.

Schmidt's rebuilding program reached its pinnacle in 1970. The Lions' offense was composed of young talent with a few veterans mixed in. The defense was a mostly-veteran group that featured a solid defensive line, a trio of outstanding linebackers, and a secondary with future Hall of Famers Lem Barney and Dick LeBeau. The one knock on the team was that some of the defensive players were getting old. Heading that list was thirty-five-year-old Alex Karras who was playing on a bad leg. It would be his final season.

Detroit was expected to compete with Minnesota for the Central Division title, and their season started well. After six games the Lions were 5-1, with their only loss coming at Washington. The Vikings were also 5-1, and showdown game #1 took place at Tiger Stadium on November 1st. Detroit kept it close during the first half and went to the locker room down 17-24. But in the second half the Vikings showed who was boss by holding the Lions scoreless. The final score was Vikings 30, Lions 17.

The New Orleans Saints were next on the schedule. An expansion team in 1967, the Saints were a league doormat. The Lions went into New Orleans expecting to win and almost did (this game is described in Chapter 10). The Saints kept the game close, then scored a huge upset when their kicker, Tom Dempsey, made NFL history by hitting a 63-yard field goal as time expired. The Lions could only watch while the jubilant Saints left the field with a 19-17 victory and Dempsey on their shoulders. The loss put the Lions at 5-3.

Showdown game #2 with Minnesota was a week later. This was an absolute must-win if the Lions were going to win the Central. Playing in Minnesota, the Lions had a 20-10 lead at the end of the third quarter and looked to be in control. But the Vikings mounted a comeback and pulled a victory out of the hat in the final minutes (see Chapter 4). The Lions dropped to 5-4 and their hopes of reaching the playoffs were about gone.

It's a testament to the fortitude of the players and coaches that they put the losing streak in the rear-view mirror and plowed ahead. They won their next game, a home victory against San Francisco who went on to win the West and reach the NFC Championship Game. Then they beat a quality Oakland Raiders team at Tiger Stadium. Next was a home win over the Cardinals on a cold day in Detroit. The Lions then flew to Los Angeles and, in their second appearance on Monday Night Football, beat the Rams 28-23 in a thriller at the Coliseum. They closed out the season by defeating the Packers 20-0 at Tiger Stadium. The Lions had won five consecutive games to finish the season 10-4.

The Vikings won the Central Division with a 12-2 record, but the Lions had the best record among NFC non-division winners. Under the new rules of the merged NFL the Lions were headed to the playoffs as the NFC's first-ever wild card team. They would go on the road to play the Eastern Division winner Dallas Cowboys. Las Vegas betting odds had Detroit as 3.0 point favorites.

The Cowboys' path to the playoffs was remarkably similar to the Lions. They were 5-2 at midseason, with one of the losses being a bone-crushing 13-54 defeat at Minnesota. That was followed by two more losses, including a 0-38 embarrassment against the Cardinals on Monday Night Football. By mid-season the Cowboys, like the Lions, looked to be out of the playoffs. But they also bounced back, went on a 5-0 run, and finished the season 10-4 which was enough to win the East. Their defense was especially strong at the end; in the final four games opponents scored a total of 15 points.

The playoff game took place on Saturday December 26th at the Cotton Bowl in Dallas in 35 degrees and under a sunny sky. Dallas kicked off to Detroit. The Lions failed to make a first down, so they punted. On the Cowboys' first possession, quarterback Craig Morton threw a pass that was tipped into the hands of Lions' safety Mike Weger. He returned the ball to the Detroit 46. On the next play, Greg Landry couldn't find an open receiver, so he started running. He was about 10 yards past the line of scrimmage when he fumbled. The ball shot forward and was grabbed by Cowboys defensive back Charlie Waters, who returned it to the Dallas 46. The Cowboys offense then moved the ball into the Detroit end, but their drive stalled on the 19-yard line. Dallas kicked a field goal to take a 3-0 lead.

Those 3 points turned out to be all the scoring Dallas needed to win the game. Both offenses were stifled by their opponents' defenses. The Lions also hurt themselves: Landry's fumble was followed by a fumble by Altie Taylor (on the Dallas 29). Larry Walton dropped a pass on the Dallas 39 that Joe Schmidt thought cost the Lions 3 points.[29] Greg Landry was 5-12 passing for 48 yards, and the Lions rushed for 76 yards. Dallas wasn't much better on offense. They had the first quarter field goal, and after that the Lions' defense held them scoreless. Quarterback Craig Morton was 4-18 passing for 38 yards. The one bright spot for the Cowboys was running back Duane Thomas who accounted for 135 of Dallas's 209 rushing yards.

The game's most exciting action took place in the fourth quarter. After the Lions punted, the Cowboys downed the ball on the their 23. Ten straight running plays—five by Duane Thomas and five by Walt Garrison—moved the ball to a first down on the Lions' 5-yard line. Three more running plays moved the ball to the 6-inch line. The Cowboys went for it on fourth down. Morton handed the ball to Thomas, who tripped over the legs of one of his linemen and was downed on the 2. The Lions' defense had held, and just over six minutes remained.

Two Detroit running plays netted one yard, and on third down Landry dropped back into the end zone to pass. But before he could get the ball off, he was tackled by George Andrie and Jethro Pugh for a 2-point safety. It was a huge play because it put the Cowboys up 5-0; the Lions could no longer tie with a field goal.

There was 4:45 on the game clock. Following the safety, Detroit kicked to Dallas. The Cowboys couldn't get a first down and punted. The ball went into the end zone for a touchback, so it was Lions' ball on their own 20 with 2:18 remaining. They had three time-outs.

Schmidt sent Bill Munson out to quarterback the final drive. The Lions moved the ball to their 32 for a first down (their sixth of the game). Munson then threw three incompletions. On fourth down he threw again, this time downfield to Earl McCullough. McCullough made a great catch between two defenders and was tackled on the Dallas 29. Detroit called time out with 0:59 seconds left.

Munson threw more passes. The first-down play was to McCullough near the goal line, but even if he'd caught it, he would've been out of bounds. The next attempt was for Altie Taylor, but a fierce Cowboys' pass rush caused Munson to hurry the throw and miss. On third down, he threw to McCullough again, this time on a post pattern. McCullough was open near the middle of the field and Munson's pass was on target, but a tad high. McCullough reached for it, but the ball glanced off his hands and landed in the arms of the Cowboys' cornerback Mel Renfro. The Lions' season was over.

The final score was Dallas 5, Detroit 0. The game still holds the record for the lowest scoring playoff game in NFL history. Afterwards, Joe Schmidt praised the defense and said the offense had been done in by nerves and inexperience. Two fumbles, a dropped pass, and the interception cost the Lions the game.

The players were disappointed but held their heads high because they'd had a good year and were proud of the late-season winning streak. Lions' fans thought 1970 was the start of something good, that the Lions were a team on the up-and-up and would be back better than ever in 1971.

However, it was not to be. The age issue caught up with the defense in 1971. The offense scored plenty of points, but the defense went downhill and the season was a disappointment. Also, the team suffered a devastating blow on October 24th when receiver Chuck Hughes suffered a heart attack and died on the field at Tiger Stadium during a game against the Bears (see chapter 10). The Lions started 4-1, but ended the season 7-6-1 and in second place behind Minnesota. Schmidt coached the Lions again in 1972, and the result was similar: 8-5-1 and second place. He resigned at the end of the season, saying coaching wasn't fun anymore.

As a postscript, after knocking off the Lions in the 1970 playoff game, the Cowboys went on to win the NFC Championship. Their opponents in Super Bowl V were the Baltimore Colts and the game is often called the Blunder Bowl because the teams turned the ball over a total of eleven times, seven by Baltimore and four by Dallas. While not the greatest Super Bowl in NFL history, it does rank as one of the more entertaining. Baltimore won 16-13 on a last-second field goal.

1983: Wide Right in San Francisco

Following Joe Schmidt's resignation, the Lions went through three head coaches in five years. Don McCafferty, who'd coached the 1970 Baltimore Colts to the Super Bowl victory over Dallas, led the Lions to a 6-7-1 record in 1973, but then sadly died of a heart attack the following summer. Rick Forzano, an assistant coach on the team, was elevated to head coach and lasted until October 1976 when he was fired after the fourth game of the season. His record was 15-17. The replacement was Tommy Hudspeth who coached the team through the 1977 season. He was fired with an 11-13 record.

Monte Clark came next. Recommended by Don Shula, Clark had been the Dolphins' offensive line coach from 1970-73, and offensive coordinator from 1974-75. His success in Miami was the springboard to the head coaching job in San Francisco in 1976. The team had gone through three consecutive losing seasons, so when Clark coached them to an 8-6 record he was considered a "savior."[30] However, he didn't finish out his contract because in March 1977 the 49ers were sold to the DeBartolo family. They installed a general manager named Joe Thomas who was legendary around the NFL for being a one-man disaster. Wanting nothing to do with Thomas, Clark resigned and was out of the league for the 1977 season.

The Lions hired Clark in January 1978. His contract gave him the title head coach and director of player operations. In effect, he had the same deal as Joe Schmidt: he was head coach and responsible for acquiring players. General Manager Russ Thomas was in charge of signing the players to contracts.

Monte Clark ranks high among Lions head coaches for his longevity. In Lions' history, only Wayne Fontes (nine seasons) and George Wilson (eight seasons) lasted longer. Clark held the job for seven seasons and his teams went 43-63-1. While the record doesn't impress, there were a few quality seasons including 1983 when the Lions came oh-so-close.

Clark rebuilt the Lions by focusing on the offensive and defensive lines. In the 1978 draft, the Lions chose a cornerback first (Luther Bradley), then six linemen including Homer Elias, Amos Fowler, and Al "Bubba" Baker. Elias and Fowler started on the offensive line for several seasons, and Baker was a key member of the Lions' Silver Rush defensive line of the late 1970s and early 1980s.

The 1978 team went 7-9, and then disaster struck in 1979. The injury bug hit the Lions during the preseason and they never recovered. They lost several starters, including quarterback Gary Danielson who was out for the year. The team went 2-14, but there was one piece of good news: since the Lions were the worst team in the NFL, they had the number one pick in the 1980 draft.[31] This mattered because most everyone in the NFL thought University of Oklahoma running back Billy Sims stood a notch above all other college draft-eligible players.

The Lions selected Sims and after a six-week contract dispute he was ready to wear a Lions' uniform. Sims added a great deal to the Detroit offense. He scored thirteen rushing TDs, gained 1,303 yards on the ground, and won NFL Offensive Rookie of the Year. Both the Lions and Vikings finished the season with 9-7 records, but Minnesota was declared the Central Division winner because they had the better record against NFC teams. It was a setback for the Lions, but their future looked bright.

1981 was another what-might-have-been season. Gary Danielson dislocated his wrist in week 4, and at the end of week 6 the Lions were 2-4. Monte Clark decided to try Eric Hipple at quarterback, and then the team started to win. Over the next nine games the Lions were 6-3, and the season came down to a finale that mattered. Detroit and Tampa Bay were tied for first in the Central with identical 8-7 records and—as luck would have it—were playing each other at the Silverdome in the last game of the season. The victor would win the Central, and the loser's season would be over. Unfortunately, as has happened so many times over the years, the Lions failed in the clutch. Miscues cost them the game: a missed field goal, a dropped pass, and giving up an 84-yard touchdown pass. The Buccaneers won 20-17 and went on to reach the NFC title game which they lost to the Rams.

Clarks' fifth year was the 1982 strike season. The Lions went 4-5 which earned the last playoff seed (#8) in the NFC (division races were thrown out that year). In the first round they were matched against #1 seed Washington (who went on to win the Super Bowl) and were soundly defeated 7-31. The Lions turned the ball over five times.

Clark's best team was in 1983, but it didn't look like it early on. The Lions won the opener against Tampa Bay, then proceeded to lose the next four. There was widespread speculation that Clark was about to get fired, and he seemed to think so too. After the fourth loss he told reporters "I'll see you at the cemetery."[32]

A week later, owner Bill Ford told a reporter he wasn't thinking about changing coaches. He also did something he'd never done while owning the team: he attended the pregame breakfast and spoke to the assembled group. He expressed confidence they were a good team, and urged them to have more fun.[33] His appearance was seen as a vote of confidence in Clark. Afterwards, the Lions went out and dismantled the Packers by a score of 38-14. "We're the same team as before," Clark said afterwards. "We just didn't have the mistakes."[34]

It was the turning point of the season. The Lions proceeded to go 7-3 the rest of the way, including key wins against Chicago, Minnesota, and Green Bay. Each of those teams ended the season 8-8 which put them one game behind the Lions (9-7) in the division. The Lions won the Central because they pulled off a late-season run and were 7-1 against divisional opponents.

The Lions were the #3 seed in the NFC which gave them a bye in the first round, and sent them on the road against #2 seed San Francisco in the divisional round. The 49ers had won their first Super Bowl two seasons before, then missed the playoffs in 1982. Now they were back in contention as Western Division champs with a 10-6 record.

The game was played on December 31st under a clear sky but the field was wet from rain earlier in the week. Lions' starting quarterback Eric Hipple was out due to a knee injury, so Gary Danielson started. His day began horribly, then improved. Mistakes ultimately cost the Lions the game and Danielson made his share. He also led a second half comeback that came up just-short.

Detroit was ahead 3-0 in the first quarter when Danielson threw his first interception. The Lions were on the 49ers' 26-yard line when 49ers' defensive back Ronnie Lott (HOF) intercepted. He was downed on the 15. San Francisco's offense then marched 85 yards for a touchdown and a 7-3 lead. On the first play of the Lions' next possession, Danielson threw interception number two. Linebacker Riki Ellison, who intercepted twice during the game, caught the ball and was tackled on the Lions' 24. The 49ers scored another touchdown to make it 14-3.

Interceptions three and four came in the second quarter, but both times the Lions' defense held the 49ers to field goal attempts. Kicker Ray Wersching missed from 38 and 35 yards. The Lions offense had a great chance when Billy Sims broke a 56-yard run along the right sideline.

He was near the goal line when Eric Wright knocked him out of bounds on the 4. After the game Sims said he didn't see Wright until the last second and had he known would've dived for the goal line and, he thought, scored a touchdown. In a game of key moments this was a big one because the Lions ended up settling for a field goal by Eddie Murray. Detroit hit one more field goal, a 54-yarder by Murray at the end of the half. The Lions trailed 9-14.

Danielson's fifth and final interception came in the third quarter and gave the 49ers the ball on the Lions' 45. The 49ers' offense advanced the ball to the Lions' 2 where they were stopped. Their field goal made the score 17-9.

Gary Danielson somehow transformed himself into a super quarterback for the rest of the game. Late in the third quarter, he went 6-6 passing on a 73-yard drive which Billy Sims finished by running eleven yards into the end zone for a touchdown. The extra point made the score San Francisco 17, Detroit 16.

The Lions had another chance when the 49ers fumbled and linebacker Gerry Cobb recovered on the San Francisco 37. But the Lions couldn't do much on offense and attempted a 43-yard field goal. Murray missed wide left.

Yet another chance came moments later. On the 49ers' third play following the Lions' field goal miss, Bobby Watkins intercepted a Joe Montana pass and returned the ball to the San Francisco 26. Five straight running plays, capped by Billy Sims' five yarder to the end zone, gave the Lions a touchdown and the lead. The extra point made the score Detroit 23, San Francisco 17. There was 4:54 remaining.

A big reason why Joe Montana is considered one of the greatest NFL quarterbacks of all-time is because of his ability to lead his team on late fourth-quarter game-winning scoring drives. When the pressure was on, Montana was at his best. He led comeback drives in regular season games, playoff games, and Super Bowls. One such drive that helped build his legend occurred against the Lions in 1983.

The Lions kicked off and the 49ers started on their 30-yard line. San Francisco worked the ball down the field, mixing runs and passes, going 70 yards in nine plays, all the while using up the clock. The Lions couldn't stop them. The drive ended with a 14-yard touchdown pass to Freddie Solomon, and Wersching's extra point put the 49ers on top, 24-23. The clock read 1:23.

The Lions received the kickoff and started on their own 26 with three time-outs. Danielson was sacked for a loss, then moved the ball down the field by dodging rushers and completing passes to Jeff Chadwick, Freddie Scott (who caught two), and Leonard Thompson. The final play was a run by Billy Sims who was tackled at the 49ers' 24-yard line. The Lions called time out with 0:11 left.

Eddie Murray came onto the field to attempt a 42-yard field goal to win the game. When the Lions' time-out expired, San Francisco called one to ice Murray. Moments before the ball was snapped, Monte Clark prayed on the sidelines while the fans at Candlestick Park screamed. The snap was good, Murray kicked, and the ball was in the air.

"I even jumped up and started celebrating," said Monte Clark. "Even after he kicked it."[35]

Ray Wersching, the 49ers' kicker who missed two field goals that day and blamed it on the field conditions, didn't watch the flight of the ball. Instead, he watched Murray: "The field was much softer and spongier than it appeared. I thought Murray was going to make it, but when he planted his left [non-kicking] foot, it gave way and I figured he might push it to the right. And he did."[36]

The ball had plenty of distance but sailed just wide of the right goalpost. Clark later said his prayer was answered, but the answer was "no."

In the locker room afterwards, several Lions blamed themselves for the loss. Gary Danielson apologized to teammates for the five interceptions. Billy Sims regretted not diving for the end zone on the sideline run. Bobby Watkins bemoaned getting beaten on the Freddie Solomon touchdown pass. Eddie Murray felt awful about the two missed field goals, especially the last one: "I led it to the right. If I had a hara-kiri knife, I would have committed it right there. Everything we've been working for as a team went down the drain."[37]

The Lions packed up and left for the airport, but their hellish New Year's Eve wasn't over. Their charter flight took off but the plane soon had mechanical problems and had to dump fuel over San Francisco Bay before returning to San Francisco for an emergency landing.[38] The team rang in the New Year at the airport while waiting for another flight, and finally arrived in Detroit after dawn.

There are many what-ifs about that playoff loss. If the field goal had been successful, would the Lions have reached the Super Bowl? They were a talented team on a hot streak so they had a chance. However, they would've had to defeat the Redskins in Washington DC which is something the Detroit Lions have never done.

Perhaps a victory in San Francisco would have put the Lions on a different trajectory. Many 49ers' fans are convinced that The Catch, the improbable touchdown pass from Joe Montana to Dwight Clark in the 1981 NFC title game against Dallas, was the event that launched the San Francisco dynasty of the 1980s and 1990s. The Catch not only put the 49ers in Super Bowl XVI, it was followed by years of excellence that included four more Super Bowl wins over the next fourteen years. Many believe: no catch, no dynasty.

Lions' offensive lineman Keith Dorney thinks that if Eddie Murray's field goal had gone through the uprights, something similar might've happened to the Lions:

> We had a great defense. Our running attack was awesome, with a solid offensive line, and one of the best running backs, if not the best, of that era, Billy Sims, running behind us. We had a talented receiving corps, and a very underrated quarterback in Danielson.
>
> Who knows what we could have done. A Super Bowl appearance, even a victory, was a definite possibility. Given that success, the Lions might not have fired one of the best, if not the best, coaches in the league at the time, Monte Clark, and maybe I wouldn't have had to endure one humiliating losing season after another for the rest of my career.
>
> Maybe we would have made it to a couple of Super Bowls. And maybe my teammates and I would have made a few more Pro Bowls. And who knows, maybe the Hall of Fame.

We'll never know if Dorney was right about Super Bowls for the Lions, but he was certainly on-target about Monte Clark. The Lions' coach was a clear casualty of the missed field goal. The criticism of Clark was that while his teams were competitive in the division, they couldn't take the next step. The Lions almost won the Central in 1980 and 1981, just qualified for the playoffs in 1982, then won the Central in 1983 but couldn't win the playoff game. Close, but not quite there. Had the field goal been good the criticism of Clark would have been silenced and he likely would've had a much longer tenure with the team.[39]

Clark was back for the 1984 season, but the team never caught stride. The season started with a quarterback controversy and a 1-5 record. Injuries took their toll. Offensive tackle Rich Strenger injured his knee in the first quarter of the opener and was lost for the season. Center

Steve Mott's knee had been injured in the 1983 playoff game and was slow to recover; he played in just six games in 1984. On October 21st in Minneapolis, Billy Sims suffered a career-ending knee injury. The season spiraled downward; over the final eight games they went 1-6-1 to finish the season 4-11-1. There was no strong case to be made for keeping Monte Clark, so he was fired on December 19, 1984.[40]

1991: One Game Away

Clark was replaced by a face familiar to many Lions fans: Darryl Rogers, who'd been the head coach at Michigan State from 1976-1979. His exit from MSU was controversial because there were three years left on his contract when he departed to take the head coaching job at Arizona State. It didn't help that he kept denying he was leaving MSU until the day ASU announced his hiring. The Lions signed him to a contract in February 1985, and his tenure did not go well. He was fired during the 1988 season with an 18-42 record.

A few notable events occurred during Rogers' time as head coach. The first is that General Manager Russ Thomas took a more active role in the team. According to newspaper reports, Thomas was responsible for hiring Rogers' offensive coordinator, a Buccaneers' assistant coach named Wayne Fontes. Thomas also hired Darrel "Mouse" Davis to install the Run and Shoot Offense (see below). Rogers denied that Thomas was hiring assistant coaches, but the *Detroit Free Press* thought the story had enough substance to print. Fontes would go on to become Rogers' replacement.

Darryl Rogers and his coaching staff chose Reggie Rogers (no relation) as the Lions' first pick in the 1987 draft. While it was a productive draft (they also selected Jerry Ball, Dennis Gibson, and Dan Saleaumua), Reggie Rogers ranks as perhaps the worst first-round pick the Detroit Lions have ever made. A highly-rated defensive lineman from the University of Washington, Rogers had psychiatric and substance abuse issues. His mental problems caused him to play in just six games during his rookie season. Then, on October 20, 1988, during his second year with the team, he was legally drunk when he drove his Jeep Cherokee through a red light in downtown Pontiac and slammed into a car carrying three teenage boys. All three boys died and Rogers's neck was broken. He was released by the Lions and spent thirteen months in prison for vehicular manslaughter.

Setting aside the Reggie Rogers pick, the Lions drafted several top players during the late 1980s who formed the foundation of the 1991 team. In 1988, while Darryl Rogers was still coach, they drafted safety Bennie Blades, linebacker Chris Spielman, safety William White, and offensive lineman Eric Aldolsek. Wayne Fontes oversaw the 1989 draft selections of running back Barry Sanders, offensive lineman Mike Utley, cornerback Ray Crockett, and quarterback Rodney Peete.[41] The 1990 draft brought quarterback Andre Ware, defensive linemen Dan Owens and Marc Spindler, and wide receiver Willie Green.[42] In 1991, they landed wide receiver Herman Moore.

When Wayne Fontes took over head coaching duties late in the 1988 season the Lions were near the bottom. Darryl Rogers' last game with the Lions was a loss to Tampa Bay witnessed by about 25,000 fans at the Silverdome. The offense was anemic; during the season the team scored 220 points which works out to an average of 13.75 per game. The Lions weren't just bad, they were boring.

The Run and Shoot was installed in 1989 as a way to perk up the offense. Mouse Davis, the new quarterbacks and receivers coach, had helped develop the scheme and used it with great success at Portland State University and then in the Canadian Football League. The offense spread around the college ranks, but had yet to be adopted by an NFL team. Shortly after Davis took the Lions' job, Fontes told him: "I want some kind of approach that puts the ball in the air and…creates some excitement. We've got to have that Ooo-oooh! Play…when the ball is thrown long and even if we miss it, the fans can go, Ooo-oooh!"[43]

The Run and Shoot, which the Lions called the Stretch Offense, uses five linemen (no tight end), a quarterback, running back, and four wide receivers. The running back can carry the ball or block a pass rusher before releasing and setting up for a screen play. The wide receivers go out for passes and adjust their patterns depending on how they're covered. For example, if the defender lines up to cover the receiver toward the inside of the field, the receiver runs to the outside. With four receivers adjusting their routes to get away from defenders, *somebody* will be open. If the quarterback is good at reading coverages and can throw passes quickly and accurately, then short-to-medium-range passes can be completed with consistency. If the offensive line can hold off the pass rush long-enough, the quarterback can throw deep. The offense is complicated, uses lots of audibles at the line of scrimmage, is designed to move the ball down the field quickly, and requires a fleet of quick receivers.[44]

The offense has drawbacks. Designed for the open field, it is less effective when the line of scrimmage is near the goal line. As the field shortens, there's less room for receivers to maneuver, plus the pass defenders are packed into a smaller space. The offense becomes harder to execute and is prone to tipped passes and interceptions. It also doesn't deal well with short-yardage situations where a strong running game works better. Yet another problem is that the pass-oriented offense doesn't do a good job of running time off the game clock which is important for protecting fourth quarter leads. Richie Pettibone, Washington's defensive coordinator in the early 1990s, summed up some of these problems when he said the Run and Shoot came up short in two skills a team needs to win consistently: "control the clock and be able to run when you have to run."[45] He also noted that while a defense can't stop the offense, "it stops itself with turnovers."[46]

To operate the scheme during the 1989 season, the Lions signed quarterback Bob Gagliano from the USFL and drafted Rodney Peete. Their passing targets were several small, quick wide receivers and rookie running back Barry Sanders.

The Stretch Offense clearly impacted on the Lions' ability to score points. Here are the number of points scored by the average NFL team, along with the points scored for (PF) and against (PA) the Lions from 1988-1992:

SEASON	NFL AVG SCORING/TEAM	LIONS' PF*	LIONS' PA*	PF-PA
1988	325	220	313	-93
1989	330	312	364	-52
1990	322	373	413	-40
1991	304	339	295	+44
1992	299	273	332	-59

* PF = points for, PA = points against.

The 220 points scored by the Lions in 1988 was 105 fewer than the NFL team average. The Lions' record that season was 4-12. The Stretch Offense and running back phenom Barry

Sanders were in place for 1989, and the Lions scored 312 points, and then 373 in 1990, a remarkable gain of 153 points over two years. During those two seasons Sanders accounted for 3,536 yards of offense and scored 30 touchdowns. He credits the offense, which spread out defenders, for helping him achieve those numbers.[47] However, while the Lions' win/loss record was better than in 1988 (7-9 in 1989, 6-10 in 1990), they remained a losing team. The reason why can be seen in the column showing points scored against the Lions. The offense was scoring more points, but the defense was giving up more too.

Many observers thought the new offense had a lot to do with the Lions' worsening defensive performance. As noted earlier, the Run and Shoot isn't conducive to controlling the game clock. The offense moves the ball down the field quickly, with occasional incomplete passes stopping the clock. As a result, offensive drives tend to be of short duration which doesn't give the defensive unit much time to rest. As a game wears on, defenders can get fatigued and yield more yards and points. In 1989, the first full season the Lions used the Stretch, their average time of possession per game was 25.78 minutes. There are 60:00 minutes in a regulation game, so the opposition held the ball an average of 34.22, or 8:44 longer per game. Only once, in the fifteenth game of the season, did the Lions keep the ball longer than their opponent.[48]

Prior to the start of the 1991 season, virtually no one predicted success for the Lions. In fact, oddsmaker Danny Sheridan said it was 6-1 odds that Wayne Fontes would be fired before the season was over. Football sages acknowledged that Detroit possessed young talent and would score points, but the defensive personnel which had allowed opponents to score so many points in 1990 was returning largely intact (seven starters returned in 1991). Furthermore, the team hadn't enjoyed a winning record since 1983. Why would 1991 be any different?

In fact, changes had taken place during the offseason that would benefit the Lions enormously. The watershed event that stirred the pot was an atrocious 38-41 overtime loss to Washington on November 4, 1990. It was a game the Lions dominated well into the third quarter, at one point holding a 35-14 lead. Then Washington went on a scoring rampage and tied the game with 0:18 remaining. They kicked a field goal in overtime to win. During the fourth quarter, when the Lions needed to hold the ball and use up the clock, they couldn't do it. The offensive troubles continued during the overtime period. From the start of the fourth quarter to the end of the game, the Lions gained 17 yards of offense and never handed the ball to Barry Sanders. During one possession they ran three consecutive pass plays that used 0:19. The defense couldn't do anything right either: Washington's last two touchdown drives were 80 and 85 yards. Over the entire game, the Lions' defense gave up 674 yards and 39 first downs. Washington ran 109 offensive plays to the Lions 46 and held the ball 49:52 to the Lions 19:18. The Run and Shoot's flaws were exposed.

"It was the turning point of our season," Chris Spielman said later. Rodney Peete added: "It's a game we never, ever should have lost. I think about it all the time. It's a game that lingers in everybody's mind."[49] Before kickoff, the Lions were 3-4 and hopeful they could make a late-season run for the playoffs. When Washington's game-winning field goal sailed through the uprights those thoughts were erased and the players' confidence was crushed. They finished the season 6-10.

The debacle led to two important changes that contributed to the Lions' success in 1991. First, Coach Wayne Fontes decided the offense had to be modified. He wanted more running plays, a tight end added to the scheme, and larger receivers. Mouse Davis—a Run and Shoot purist—disagreed so he and the Lions parted ways. The second major change was in defensive strategy. The players persuaded Fontes that the defense should be more attack-oriented, as opposed to Fontes's philosophy of "bend-don't-break." The team had been playing a 3-4 defense and relying on pass defenders to not give up big plays. In 1991, the Lions used a more aggressive pass rush, in some games employing four linemen instead of three. This defensive strategy, along with an emphasis on creating turnovers and added game experience for young players, helps explain why the Lions gave up 118 fewer points in 1991 than in 1990.

However, none of these positives showed up in the Lions' first game of the season. They opened against the Redskins in Washington DC and the Lions were overmatched from the start. Washington scored touchdowns on their first three possessions, led 35-0 at halftime, and won the game 45-0. The season had begun with a great big thud.

The opening day loss didn't exactly fire up Lions fans: the following week only 43,132 were at the Silverdome for the home opener against the Packers. To everyone's surprise, a different Lions' team showed up. This one played with fire, didn't turn the ball over, and left the field with a 23-14 victory. They did it again a week later, this time at home against the Dolphins. The 17-13 win included a goal line stand at the end to secure the victory. In both games the Lions held the ball longer than their opponents. Fontes's new-look offense and more aggressive defense seemed to be working.

The Lions won their next three: on the road at Indianapolis, then at home against Tampa Bay and Minnesota. The victory over the Vikings (described in Chapter 4) was especially inspiring because the Lions were down 17 points with 8:38 left in the game. They staged one of the greatest late-game comebacks in Lions' history, capped by Barry Sanders' game-winning 15-yard touchdown run with 0:36 second left. The victory put the Lions at 5-1.

The bye-week was next, followed by a midseason slump. The Lions lost at San Francisco 3-35, then came home and defeated the Cowboys 34-10. It was a costly win, however, because starting quarterback Rodney Peete tore his Achilles tendon on the Lions' first possession and was lost for the season. Erik Kramer, who played in the CFL before coming to the Lions, quarterbacked the Lions to victory. The Lions lost their next two—both on the road—to Chicago and Tampa Bay. They were 6-4, and two games behind the 8-2 Chicago Bears.

What followed was a remarkable 6-0 winning streak. They beat the Rams on November 17th in a game best remembered for Mike Utley's tragic injury. Utley suffered two broken vertebrae in his neck and was permanently paralyzed when his head hit the Silverdome turf. While being wheeled away on a gurney he gave a thumps-up signal; his teammates dedicated the rest of the season to their fallen comrade. The Lions defeated the Vikings in Minnesota, then faced off against the Bears on Thanksgiving Day. It was a huge game in the standings, and before a sellout crowd at the Silverdome the Bears turned the ball over six times and the Lions prevailed 16-6. Following wins against the Jets and Packers (their last win in Green Bay until 2015), the team prepared for the season finale against the Bills in Buffalo. Going into the final weekend both the Lions and Bears were 11-4, but the Bears held the first tiebreaker because they had a better record in the division.

The Bills rested some of their starters, but that didn't make the Lions' 17-14 overtime victory any less satisfying. When the Bears lost in San Francisco later that day the Detroit Lions were Central Division champions. As the NFC's #2 playoff seed they would host a playoff game for the first time since 1957.

It was a shocking outcome. At the start of the season almost no one predicted major success for the Lions. Not only did they win their division, they did so in the face of enormous adversity. Wide receiver Aubrey Matthews was lost on opening day, linebacker Mike Cofer (the team's sack leader the previous three seasons) played in just two games, quarterback Rodney Peete's season ended in the eighth game, offensive guard Mike Utley's career was over in the eleventh game, and nose tackle Jerry Ball and offensive tackle Eric Sanders were lost in the fourteenth game.[50] The Lions kept winning because they were loaded with talent (there were seven Pro-Bowlers), had able replacements, and played with enthusiasm and confidence.

The modified offensive and defensive schemes Fontes had installed achieved their goals. The offense did a better job of controlling the clock and the attack-oriented defense was able to get the opposition's offense off the field sooner. During the 1991 season the Lions held the ball longer than eight opponents.

A key to the Lions' success was their level of play in domed stadiums. They were 10-0 indoors—eight wins in Pontiac, plus road wins at Indianapolis and Minneapolis. It was a different story outdoors where they were 2-4, winning at Green Bay and Buffalo. Here are numbers that illustrate the point:[51]

1991 DETROIT LIONS REGULAR SEASON

	Indoors	Outdoors
Record	10-0	2-4
Points Scored/Game	27	12
Points Allowed/Game	13	27
Takeaway/Giveaway[52]	+19	-11
Lions' Pass Completion Rate	57.7%	49.5%
Opponents' Pass Completion Rate	57.4%	63.5% [52]

Indoors the Lions scored more points, gave up fewer points, won the turnover battle, had a better passing game, and were better at defending the pass. One reason why is that the team was built on speed which made sense because the Pontiac Silverdome had the hardest, fastest playing surface in the NFL. Some of that speed advantage was lost outdoors, especially on natural grass fields. The Lions played five outdoor games on natural grass that season, and their lone win was in Green Bay. The other outdoor victory (in Buffalo) was on artificial turf.

Not surprisingly, the indoor/outdoor tendencies carried over to the playoffs. The Lions' playoff games were against teams they'd seen during the regular season and in the same venues. They defeated the Cowboys at the Silverdome both times by similar scores, and lost the two road games to Washington by similar scores.

DATE	REG/PLAYOFF	VENUE	SCORE
10/27/1991	Regular Season	Silverdome	Det 34, Dallas 10
1/5/1992	Playoff	Silverdome	Det 38, Dallas 6
9/1/1991	Regular Season	RFK Stadium	Wash 45, Det 0
1/12/1992	Playoff	RFK Stadium	Wash 41, Det 10

The Lions' home playoff game was against the Cowboys on January 5, 1992. The Lions had beaten them at the Silverdome on October 27th by a score of 34-10. In that game the Lions ran the ball twenty-eight times, with Barry Sanders accounting for twenty-one of the attempts. The running game wasn't especially productive (72 yards total, 55 by Sanders), but it opened up the passing game. Erik Kramer was 9-16 with two touchdowns. The Lions also scored on a blocked field goal attempt that was recovered and run into the end zone by William White, and a 96-yard pick-six interception return by Ray Crockett.

Lions' fans' excitement level for the playoff game was sky-high. The faithful hoped for a repeat of what had taken place in October, and it happened although in a different way. After forcing a punt on Dallas' opening possession, the Lions came out passing. The coaches thought the Cowboys would be expecting a steady dose of Barry Sanders so they changed things up by having Kramer throw early. The first drive consisted of four completions on five attempts, the final one being a 31-yard throw to Willie Green in the end zone. On the Lions' next possession they threw four more passes before finally handing off to Sanders. That drive stalled, but the Lions scored again in the second quarter when Mel Jenkins had a pick-six interception. The PAT made the score 14-3. After that, the Lions were off to the races. The first half passes opened up second-half runs, and the final nail in the Cowboys' coffin was an astounding 47-yard TD run by Barry Sanders in the fourth quarter. Sanders was nearly tackled, emerged from the pile, and then dashed past stunned defenders on his way to the goal line. It was the icing on the cake of a fabulous day, a 38-6 victory that is the Lions' greatest moment since 1957. It was a major setback for Dallas but hold the tears because the following season they won their first of three Super Bowls in four years.

The victory put the Lions on the road against the #1 seed Washington Redskins who had destroyed them 45-0 on opening day. Washington was the best team in the NFL that year, having ended the regular season 14-2 and eventually winning the Super Bowl. Today, the 1991 Redskins are considered one of the greatest NFL teams of all-time. The cards were stacked against the Lions: the game was outdoors, the second-half was played in rain, the boisterous crowd made it hard to call audibles, and Detroit's linemen didn't match up well against Washington's linemen. The Lions knew it would be an uphill battle, but thought they had a chance because they'd played so well late in the season.

The game started badly for the Lions. The Lions took the kickoff and began deep in their own end. The first offensive play was a tipped pass that was called back on an illegal procedure penalty. On the second play, Kramer dropped back to pass and was hit at the 10-yard line by defensive end Charles Mann. Kramer fumbled, Washington recovered on the 11, and two plays later (and 66 seconds into the game) Gerald Riggs scored on a 2-yard run. A short while afterwards (four minutes into the game) Washington kicked a field goal and the Lions were down 10-0.

The Lions mounted a bit of a comeback in the second quarter. Kramer hit Willie Green for an 18-yard TD pass, but then Washington scored another touchdown. The Lions' final points came on a field goal before halftime. The teams headed to the locker room with Washington leading 17-10.

The second half was all Washington. As had happened on opening day, the Lions were manhandled at the line of scrimmage and held scoreless while Washington's offense continued to rack up yards and points. When Fontes replaced Kramer with Andre Ware, it didn't make a difference. The final blow to the Lions was a pick-six interception by Washington's star cornerback Darrell Green (HOF). During the game, Detroit turned the ball over three times and their quarterbacks were sacked five times. Washington committed no turnovers and took no sacks. The final score was Washington 41, Detroit 10.

By the time the Lions and their equipment were loaded onto the team buses, the rain had turned to snow. As the buses were leaving the stadium Wayne Fontes saw Bill and Martha Ford standing on a street corner. He had the driver stop, and then left the bus and asked the Fords if they wanted to come inside and wait for their ride. The Fords declined, then Fontes apologized for the team's play.

"[Mr. Ford] said 'I understand…maybe next year,' Fontes recalled. "He…or…his…wife, one of them, said 'This is the best we've done in years and it's been a great run.' I was down and he was down, and when we stood there in the snow together…somebody should have painted it [because] it would have made a great picture."[53]

As in 1970, the Lions and their fans thought the playoff year was the start of something good. There was continued success, but not at the level fans and ownership hoped for. The team was near the top of the league but seemed cursed. Mike Utley had been paralyzed in November, then during the offseason tragedy struck twice. In May 1992, defensive backfield coach Len Fontes (head coach Wayne Fontes's brother) died of a heart attack. Then in June starting offensive lineman Eric Andolsek was hit by a truck and killed while pulling weeds in front of his home in Louisiana. The team slipped badly in 1992, falling to 5-11, but bounced back in 1993 to win the Central. They hosted another playoff game, the heartbreaking loss to the wild card Packers when Brett Favre threw the game-winning touchdown pass to a wide-open Sterling Sharpe in the final minute. The Lions reached the playoffs as wild cards the next two seasons, but lost in Green Bay in 1994 and in 1995 suffered the blowout loss in Philadelphia. Fontes was back for the 1996 season but the team went 5-11 and missed the playoffs. He was fired on December 26, 1996.

Wayne Fontes was gone but not forgotten because he will long be remembered as the coach who had the Lions one win away from the Super Bowl.

Chapter 3
Russ Thomas: A GM Worth Remembering

John Russell ("Russ") Thomas (1924-1991) enjoyed a long career with the Detroit Lions. Born in West Virginia, he played collegiate football at Ohio State University during the mid-1940s, and was the Lions' third-round pick in the 1946 draft. An offensive and defensive tackle, his playing career ended in 1949 due to a knee injury. He moved on to coaching and was an assistant at St. Bonaventure before serving as a Lions' assistant coach during the championship seasons of 1952 and 1953. He moved up the organizational ladder serving as scout, broadcaster, and director of player personnel. Then, in 1967, he was appointed general manager. He held that position until 1989 when he retired after reaching the Lions' mandatory retirement age of sixty-five.

By any objective measure of on-field performance, Thomas's twenty-three-year tenure as general manager was a failure. During that time the Lions enjoyed five winning seasons and reached the playoffs three times. Coaches came and went, players came and went, but Thomas remained. An entire generation of Lions' fans considered him a big reason for the Lions' lack of success and scratched their heads in wonderment over how he kept his job.

The answer, of course, revolved around Lions' owner William Clay ("Bill") Ford (1924-2014). Bill Ford was the son of Edsel and Eleanor Ford and grandson of Henry and Clara Ford. The youngest of four children, Bill and brothers Henry and Benson became managers at Ford Motor. The oldest, Henry II (known around Detroit as "Hank the Deuce"), ran the company and was a chip of his grandfather's block in the sense that he was a ruthless tyrant who didn't care whose feet he stomped on. Bill and Benson held management positions but were second fiddles to the Deuce. Benson was in charge of dealer relations and Bill was tasked with coming up with a new version of the Lincoln Continental. The original Continental Mark I was a pathbreaking automobile designed by his father Edsel during the 1930s. Edsel, who died in 1943, is considered one of the greatest car designers who ever lived and the Mark I was his masterpiece. It was a great honor for Bill to be placed in charge of working up the Mark II version. He inherited his father's flair for design and was given a staff and sufficient resources. Unfortunately for Bill, as the project was nearing completion in the mid-1950s, Henry II was turning Ford Motor into a publicly-held corporation. Henry thought the Mark II would lose money and didn't want to have to tell that to new shareholders so he downgraded the project. Bill's autonomy was revoked and the best features of the car were removed and put in the new Ford Thunderbird. According to author John Bacon, this was a key event in Bill Ford's life: he'd been given his big chance at success but his legs were chopped out from under him before he'd been able to achieve it. He stayed with the company but grew angry, bored, and resentful toward his oldest brother. In despair, Bill took to the bottle and the alcohol abuse went on for several years. He later said that during that time, above all else, he needed something to do.[54]

Ford was a huge sports fan and especially enjoyed football. He had Lions' season tickets and often traveled to watch their road games. His involvement in the team's management occurred during an internal squabble between two of the owners, Edwin J. Anderson and D. Lyle Fife. Anderson served as president and general manager and was drawing an annual salary of $40,000, while Fife had been the team president in the late 1940s. Discord had existed between the men for years and it came out in the open in the early 1960s when Fife tried to oust Anderson from management.[55] Fife didn't think an owner should be drawing a salary and thought Anderson had done a poor job of signing draft picks. This was the era when the new American Football League (AFL) was competing with the NFL for players. In the 1960 draft the Lions selected Johnny Robinson (HOF) in the first round, but lost him to the AFL.[56] It happened again in the 1962 draft, only this time the Lions lost their first *three* picks (including John Hadl) to the AFL. In his defense, Anderson said that all three of the draftees had been dishonest during contract negotiations; they'd signed AFL contracts *before* being drafted and hadn't told the Lions. The Lions' players were so upset about losing the draftees that prior to a practice at Tiger Stadium they hanged Anderson in effigy from the south goalpost.[57]

In the midst of the drama, Anderson was countering Fife by appointing members to the Board of Directors who did not have ownership stakes but were friendly to Anderson. Bill Ford was apparently one of these people, and that served as his entrée into Lions' management. Sometime afterwards he purchased a minority stake in the team.[58] Then in January 1961, likely in an effort to stave off the Lyle Fife contingent, Ford replaced Anderson as president of the Lions. Anderson kept the GM title and his $40,000 salary.

That was the situation in October 1963 when at a Board of Directors' meeting Ford offered to buy out the other owners for $4.5 million. The directors were interested, and during the next month there was much discussion while voting proxies from the 140-plus owners were gathered. The next board meeting was held at Detroit's Statler Hilton Hotel on November 22, 1963, and Ford's buyout offer was accepted. At a celebratory lunch in the hotel's restaurant afterwards, a waitress asked Ford if he'd heard about President Kennedy.[59] The tragic news snuffed out the festive atmosphere and the day ended with President Kennedy dead and the pathway clear for Bill Ford to become sole owner of the Detroit Lions. The deal was finalized in January 1964.[60]

Some years earlier Bill Ford and Russ Thomas had formed a friendship and it lasted until Thomas's death in 1991. The details aren't clear, but an oft-told story is that they were drinking buddies and Thomas was the guy who made sure Ford got home safely. Another story is that once Ford conquered his addiction, Thomas was there to make sure his friend didn't fall off the wagon. Whatever the case, upon taking ownership in 1964, one of Ford's first moves was to appoint Thomas as director of player personnel. Then, in early 1967, he promoted Thomas to general manager.

The Management Team

Bill Ford and Russ Thomas made an odd pairing because those who knew them were left with completely different impressions. Ford was widely liked, Thomas widely disliked.

Ford is described as nice; loyal; generous; private; unpretentious. Born into enormous wealth, he didn't lord it over people. He insisted everyone call him Bill. During summers home from college he worked as an assembly line worker at Ford's Rouge Plant in Dearborn. He drove himself around the Detroit area in Ford cars painted Honolulu Blue. He was happily married to wife Martha and devoted to their four children.

Impressions of Russ Thomas are different: underqualified; gruff; set in his ways; cheapskate; tightwad; Ebenezer Scrooge reincarnated; son of a bitch; meddler; the Ayatolla. Jerry Argovitz, who was Billy Sims' agent, said Thomas "didn't have a humble bone in his body."[61] John Bacon describes him as "Henry [Ford] II without the smarts."[62] When asked about Thomas, former Lions' coach Joe Schmidt said, "you'll have a hard time finding anyone to say something nice about him, except his wife and kids."[63]

So why did nice guy Bill Ford (1) appoint the unpopular Russ Thomas as general manager, and (2) keep him in that position for twenty-three years while the team floundered on the field?

A large part of the answer involves their friendship. Thomas was working for the Lions when Ford took sole ownership and, according to John Bacon, Ford pledged to Thomas that he'd always have a job with the team. Loyalty—for which Ford was legendary—and friendship explain why Ford first promoted Thomas to director of player personnel and then to general manager. We don't know why Ford thought Thomas would make a good GM although given how things played out it's likely he knew Thomas would keep a lid on players' salaries.

Given the years of dismal on-field performance, how did Thomas keep the job for so long? According to many who knew Ford, his character flaw was loyalty to a fault. John Bacon believes the incident at Ford Motor—when Henry yanked the Continental Mark II project from Bill—changed Bill's life. It led him to take on a job (owning the Lions) where he had control. He then offered opportunities to others by hiring them and providing plenty of time to sink or swim. Most of them sank and he'd stick with them longer than others might've, especially if Ford felt connected to the person. Russ Thomas clearly fit in this category. If not for the Lions' mandatory retirement rule, perhaps Thomas would've been GM even longer. Lions' Hall of Famer Lem Barney said this about Ford: "some of the people he stuck with [were] not very good."[64]

There were all those head coaches: during Ford's time as owner he hired sixteen, four of whom (Don McCafferty, Monte Clark, Bobby Ross, and Jim Caldwell) had prior NFL head coaching experience. Just one (Dick Jauron) obtained another NFL head coaching job after leaving the Lions. Perhaps Ford's most bizarre hire was Matt Millen. Millen had no experience in football management and didn't approach Ford about being GM. Ford approached him, and Millen turned him down before finally accepting. And then, long after it was clear Millen wasn't working out, Ford extended his contract.

In terms of importance, Russ Thomas was Ford's most important hire because he held the general manager job for twenty-three years and thereby had a huge impact on the team. Thomas apparently believed his primary task was to hold down players' salaries so Ford could earn a profit. According to Detroit sportswriter Jerry Green, Russ Thomas saw his job as "protecting Bill Ford's mountain of money."[65] When asked why, Green (no fan of Thomas) answered: "because he was Russ Thomas." Detroit Free Press writer Curt Sylvester quoted "a source close to the Lions who said 'Russ' first objective is not to win, it's to survive and make money for Bill Ford.'"[66] In the many stories about salary disputes between Thomas and Lions' players, Thomas is rarely painted in a favorable light. In fact, he infuriated many players who dealt with him.

Thomas was a hardline negotiator who could pull it off because he was GM in a different era. The AFL, which bid against the NFL for players from 1960-1966, agreed to a common draft with the NFL beginning in 1967 which is the year Thomas became GM. Genuine free agency, where a player can sell his services to any NFL team, didn't come to the league until 1992, three years after Thomas retired.[67] Thomas was general manager between those two major events and during his tenure the NFL had various systems in place that resulted in the same outcome: players—unless traded—were tied to the team that drafted them.[68] Thus, in contract negotiations the buyer—the NFL team—had the power because the sellers—the players—had the option of accepting the teams' offers or not playing in the NFL. What else was available? The World Football League (WFL) existed from 1974-75, and the United States Football League (USFL) was in business from 1982-85, but the rest of the time the players' best alternative was the Canadian Football League (CFL) where salaries were lower than the NFL. So, for almost all of the years Thomas was the Lions' GM, the team was in the driver's seat during player negotiations. It's easy to imagine what it was like dealing with an arrogant tyrant determined to hold down salaries. Thomas made salary offers the players thought were lowball and trying to get him to raise the offer was like pulling teeth that wouldn't come out. When the contract was signed, the players were bitter. While it's natural that general managers and players are at odds with each other, Thomas seemed to have a special way of irritating players. His tactics diminished team morale which is a major reason why many Lions' head coaches resented him. Joe Schmidt summarized Thomas' influence this way: "He prevented us from winning."[69]

All NFL teams had contract disputes during the 1970s and 1980s, but the Lions were considered the league leader. Several high draft choices went through long, acrimonious negotiations. Billy Sims and Chuck Long were first-round picks that took several weeks to reach terms. Chuck Long missed nearly a month of practices; Billy Sims's contract talks went on for six-weeks. Several players under contract walked off the team during salary disputes. A slew of these incidents took place in the late 1970s and early 1980s. During the 1980 season, six Lions were holdouts at one time or another. Starting defensive lineman John Woodcock left the team in October and never returned.

Money, of course, was the core of the problem. Things were happening at the time to make the situation ripe for labor disputes. The NFL enjoyed an enormous increase in revenue during the 1970s and 1980s (which continues today). Television and professional football have been good for each other; the game carries over well to TV viewing and fans watch in droves. The success of this marriage has shown up in the amount television networks have been willing to pay the league for the rights to cover games. In 1970, the NFL signed a four-year, $156 million agreement with the networks. The NFL splits television revenue equally among teams, so the contract meant that each team received $1.5 million per year. Fast-forward to 1982 when another contract was signed; this one provided each team with $15 million per year. Thus, in twelve years the TV money for each team increased tenfold. (Under the eleven-year contract signed in 2021, each team receives an estimated $312 million per year.)[70]

Well aware that a flood of television money was landing on teams' doorsteps, the players wanted some of it. Salaries rose during the 1970s, but players thought teams could pay more given the increased revenue not just from television rights, but also radio rights, ticket sales, concessions, and merchandise.

As noted earlier, there were many contract disputes during this era and having Russ Thomas involved seemed to make it worse. An examination of a few cases illustrates the issues involved. Al "Bubba" Baker was a defensive end the Lions drafted out of Colorado State University in the second round in 1978. He was big (6'6", 265 lbs.), strong, and quick, and signed a three-year contract for a reported $50,000 per year. An exceptional pass rusher, Baker had an immediate impact. In his rookie year he sacked opposing quarterbacks twenty-three times (which set a franchise record), earned NFL Defensive Rookie of the Year, and was named to the Pro Bowl. It was a most auspicious start to an NFL career.

During the offseason Baker told the Lions he wanted more money. Russ Thomas responded by explaining that they had a strict rule (no doubt with Bill Ford's approval) about not renegotiating contracts, but the team was willing to extend his contract and provide a signing bonus of $25,000. "This was not a renegotiation," Thomas said afterwards. "We did not open his contract. His contract is the same as it was, we've just extended it."[71] Baker took the deal: for $25,000 of up-front money he'd obligated himself to the Lions for three more years at $50,000 per year. It was a bad move on Baker's part because during an era when salaries were rising the contract froze his salary for even longer and with a team that refused to renegotiate contracts.

Baker had another great season in 1979. Although the Lions missed the playoffs, Baker was once again the team's sack leader and named to the Pro Bowl.

During the 1980 offseason, Baker realized his mistake in signing the contract extension the year before. It was an expensive miscue because he found out that Tampa Bay defensive end Lee Roy Selmon was earning $230,000 a year. Baker called his own contract "unfair" and elaborated: "I'm not one who measures himself by other people's standards, but I don't think Lee Roy Selmon is five times better than I am."[72]

Baker reported to training camp but then left, saying he wouldn't be back until he had a new contract. Thomas's response: "I feel [he's] under contract. I know I'm being repetitious, but I feel [he's] under contract and [is] obligated to be on the team."[73]

Why wouldn't Thomas renegotiate Baker's contract? Because if the Lions had given Baker what he wanted by providing a new contract that paid him an amount similar to what top players at his position were earning elsewhere, the Lions' salary costs would have risen and profits fallen. Furthermore, renegotiating would've opened a can of worms in the sense that it wouldn't have stopped with Baker: every other member of the team who thought he was underpaid would've demanded a new contract. The downside for the Lions was that by not paying Baker more they had an unhappy player on the team.

Some NFL teams were more willing to augment players' salaries to maintain morale. Teams do not like to renegotiate contracts because of the can-of-worms problem. The easier method is to hand out bonuses as a way of supplementing players' salaries. In the 1970s and 1980s era of rising salaries, players who signed contracts a few years prior were often earning less than players with more recent contracts. Some teams handed out bonuses to players with older contracts and did so without being asked. It was a costly practice but made for happier players.[74]

The Lions went the bonus route to get Bubba Baker back in 1980. His holdout extended into the regular season and after sitting out opening day he demanded a trade. He was soon back on the team with a contract extension that didn't change his current salary, but would pay $200,000 for the 1983 season. He also received another $25,000 bonus. Baker had received only a small amount of what he wanted and was even more unhappy after that. Head Coach Monte Clark eventually decided the team would be better off without him so in July 1983 Baker was traded to the St. Louis Cardinals.

A few players tipped over the Lions' apple cart and no one did a better job of it than Billy Sims. The number-one pick in the 1980 draft, Sims was considered a cut above all the other draft-eligible players that year. He hired an agent named Jerry Argovitz and they were seeking big money. At a time when the highest paid Lion was quarterback Gary Danielson who earned $165,000 per year, Sims wanted a $1.0 million up-front signing bonus and $3.5 million more over four years. The Lions offered a $300,000 bonus deferred over ten years (which had a present value of about $115,000), and $100,000 per-year for three-years and $110,000 in the fourth year. The Lions and Sims were about $4 million apart.

Thomas blew up when he saw what Sims was asking for. "The rules are simple," Thomas told Sims' agent. "The salaries are slotted, based on the last year's draft, plus inflation. This deal [the Lions are offering] is better than what last year's first-overall pick received, plus some…When Billy's ready to play football, his contract—this very same one—will be ready here waiting for you. The only place Billy Sims is going to play football is right here in Detroit, and if he doesn't like it, he can get a job sweeping floors."[75]

Sims held firm and the two parties eventually met roughly in the middle. When the contract was signed six-weeks later, Sims received a $1 million bonus up front, a three-year contract worth roughly another $1 million, and a Lloyds of London insurance policy that would pay off if Sims suffered a career-ending injury (which happened in 1984; he ultimately collected $2.2 million from the policy). Sims was able to get so much because Ford and Thomas were under enormous pressure from fans to get him signed. He was the best player the team had drafted in years and fans knew he could make the difference between getting into the playoffs and not getting into the playoffs. The deal finally happened when Bill Ford bypassed his GM and called Sims' agent directly. According to Argovitz, "[Ford] explained that his friend Russ wasn't a bad man, just loyal to those who wrote his paychecks."[76]

In a 1988 interview, Ford was asked why he bought the Lions. He said: "I didn't get into [owning the Lions] to lose money. I certainly didn't get into it to make money…My intention was a love of sport, the game itself, and a very fond bond between the players and myself."[77] Ford wanted to earn a profit from owning the team but wasn't trying to *maximize* profits. His instructions to Thomas were probably something to the effect of 'try to put a good team on the field, but don't bust the bank doing it.' Thomas did his job, which helps explain why he lasted twenty-three years at it but his personality was such that he irritated most everyone (except Bill Ford) in the process.

The Monday Meetings

Joe Schmidt was one of just three head coaches Bill Ford hired but didn't fire.[78] After leading the team for six seasons, Schmidt resigned in January 1973, telling the press: "The job is no longer fun; I don't enjoy coaching any more. It has gotten to be more burden than fun."[79]

When asked about it years later, Schmidt explained that a large part of the reason why coaching the Lions stopped being fun was because of regularly-scheduled meetings with Bill Ford and Russ Thomas that took place every Monday following a game.[80] The meetings started at 6:00 PM and the purpose was to go over the film of the previous day's game. Noting that "Monday is a busy day in the NFL," Schmidt was required to sit through these second-guessing sessions, being questioned and criticized about the team's performance. He said the meetings were fine if the Lions had won, but if they'd lost the get-togethers could last until 11:30 PM.

The "mentally draining" meetings ground him down. After particularly grueling sessions he said it was hard to get up the next morning and go to work and motivate players. Schmidt did not say who dominated the conversations but we know the answer thanks to Rick Forzano who was the Lions' head coach from 1974-76. He was also subjected to the Monday meetings while head coach and said, "Russ Thomas did most of the interrogating."[81]

Causing Trouble to the End

Lions' fans were glad when Thomas retired in 1989. After twenty-three mostly futile seasons, team followers were well-aware of his reputation as a difficult negotiator who soured players' attitudes. No public retirement ceremony was held for Thomas in front of Detroit fans, no doubt because the front office knew what the reaction would be. Instead, he received his sendoff at the last game of the season in Atlanta.

Even though Thomas would be out the door when the 1989 season was over, he couldn't resist meddling to the end. The issue was his replacement. Bill Ford had made it clear there were two contenders: Chuck Schmidt and Jerry Vainisi. Schmidt (no relation to Joe) was an accountant who'd been with the Lions for several years and had risen to vice president of finance. Vainisi had been GM of the Chicago Bears from 1983-86 and was hired by the Lions in 1987 as vice president of player personnel. Prior to being hired Vainisi described Russ Thomas as "one of my best friends in the league."[82]

However, their friendship didn't survive working in the same building. A few months after joining the Lions, Vainisi became a Thomas critic and made the crucial error of criticizing Thomas to outsiders. Thomas found out and put Vainisi on his S-list. Meanwhile, Chuck Schmidt was a Thomas protégé sometimes referred to as "Little Russ." As Thomas's retirement drew near he lobbied Ford to name Schmidt as the replacement. According to columnist Mitch Albom, "[Vainisi] got stuck in a nasty web of office politics, mostly involving Russ Thomas who wanted to handpick his replacement."[83]

Thomas got his way. After he retired, Bill Ford named Chuck Schmidt executive vice president and chief operating officer. Jerry Vainisi remained VP of player personnel. Vainisi was disappointed but didn't show it publicly. He left the Lions in 1990 to head the organization that eventually morphed into NFL Europe. Thus, the man who had been a principal architect of the 1985 Super Bowl Chicago Bears was gone and Little Russ was second in command to Bill Ford.

Chapter 4
Late to the Game: Those Pesky Minnesota Vikings

When the Minnesota Vikings began play as an expansion team in 1961, the Detroit Lions had been around for three decades. The Vikings were placed in the Western Conference so beginning with their first season they met the Lions twice a year. Not surprisingly, the Lions dominated early on. They won the first five games but then the situation changed: over the next nine games the Lions' record was 4-3-2. The Vikings had improved relative to the Lions.

In fact, the Vikings hadn't just improved, they were on the brink of becoming a dominant team. General Manager Jim Finks (HOF) and Head Coach Norm Van Brocklin (HOF) had assembled a group of players that would develop into genuine stars. When Van Brocklin resigned after the 1967 season, he was replaced by Bud Grant (HOF). Grant inherited the talented group, helped augment it, and soon had a winning team. There were several great players but the four defensive linemen—Carl Eller (HOF), Gary Larsen, Jim Marshall, and Alan Page (HOF)—stood out. They formed the core of a defensive unit—known as the Purple People Eaters—that by 1969 was considered the best in football.

The Vikings' ascendency was bad news for the Lions. In 1967, the NFL split the Eastern and Western Conferences into a total of four divisions and assigned Detroit and Minnesota to the Central along with Chicago and Green Bay. Thus, the Lions' and Vikings' fortunes remained linked because they would continue to meet twice a year. The NFL also changed the playoff format: instead of having just the winners of the Eastern and Western Conferences play for the championship, the winners of the four divisions would play a two-round tournament to determine which team advanced to the Super Bowl to play the AFL Champion. The setup was changed again in 1970 when the AFL was merged into the NFL. The league was divided into two conferences, National and American, each with three divisions. For the Lions little changed: they were still in the Central Division with the same three opponents. The difference was that they could now get to the playoffs without winning the division because the new playoff scheme included a wild card team (the non-division winner with the best overall record). Regardless of the exact details of the arrangement, the Lions faced a fundamental problem: the Minnesota Vikings stood between them and the top of the Central Division.

The Vikings improved with astonishing speed. In 1967 their record was 3-8-3, and the following year it was 8-6 which was good enough to win the Central. In 1969 Minnesota became a top team, posting a 12-2 record, winning the division, and reaching Super Bowl III (which they lost to Kansas City). They maintained a high level of success for years: from 1968-1980 the Vikings won the Central Division eleven times and played in four Super Bowls.

A Hex on the Lions

Detroit's record against Minnesota since the Vikings began play in 1961 is shown below. The years are broken into subperiods to illustrate the different rates of Lions' success and failure.

DETROIT LIONS VS MINNESOTA VIKINGS, 1961-2022

YEARS	LIONS' WIN-LOSS-TIE	LIONS' WIN RATE
1961-67	9-3-2	69%
1968-80	4-22-0	15%
1981-97	14-19-0	42%
1998-2010	4-22-0	15%
2011-22	9-15-0	37%
Total (1961-2022)	40-81-2	33%

From 1961-1967, the Lions dominated the expansion-team Vikings. Then the Vikings fortunes shifted, and starting in 1968 were a much-improved team. They swept the Lions that year and it marks the start of the first dark era, a thirteen-year stretch when the Lions defeated the Vikings only four times in twenty-six attempts. From 1968-80 the Vikings were an NFL power, doing most everything right except win Super Bowls. During that same time the Lions placed second in the Central Division eight times. Only once, in 1970, did the Lions reach the playoffs, and that was as the wild card. The Lions' 15 percent win rate against Minnesota makes clear that a big reason why the Lions were coming in second was their horrific performance in head-to-head matches against the Vikings. The Lions rarely beat them and when they did it was only once per season. The organization and its fans were frustrated because many of those Lions teams had talent but couldn't beat the Vikings when it mattered. The Detroit media described the Vikings' hold over the Lions as a hex, and it did seem like something strange was at work. While some of the losses were lopsided affairs, there were several close games that the Vikings managed to win—or, if you prefer, the Lions managed to lose. Joe Schmidt's observation about "some stupid-ass thing" tripping up the Lions when they played the Vikings during his coaching days applied throughout the 1970s (examples are provided later in the chapter).

The Lions matched up better against the Vikings during the 1980s and 1990s, managing a win rate of 42 percent from 1981-97. The Lions had some quality teams in the early 1980s, and won the division for the first time in 1983. Also, Minnesota wasn't as dominant as in prior seasons. The Chicago Bears were the Central Division's powerhouse of the 1980s, winning six division titles from 1984-90, and the 1985 Super Bowl.

The Lions declined after 1983, but then a resurgence took place in the early 1990s. This is when the team had its best run since the 1950s: they won the division twice (1991 & 1993), played in the 1991 NFC title game, and reached the playoffs as wild cards in 1994, 1995, 1997, and 1999. The Green Bay Packers were the Central Division's most successful team of the 1990s, reaching three NFC title games, two Super Bowls, and winning the 1996 Lombardi Trophy.

The Lions' second dark time against Minnesota ran from 1998-2010. This one is easier to understand because the Lions were in serious decline. Almost nothing went right in Detroit during those years; their only playoff appearance was as an 8-8 wild card in 1999 and after that the scene turned grim. Matt Millen was named CEO in 2001 and the team soon headed toward the bottom. The Lions' overall record from 1998-2010 was 61-147 for a win rate of 29 percent. The Lions had trouble beating any team, much less the Vikings who were in the playoffs six times and played in three NFC title games. Minnesota's 1998 team went 15-1 and famously missed going to the Super Bowl because of a failed field goal attempt. In the 2009 NFC title game, the Vikings, with Brett Favre (HOF) at quarterback, took the Saints to overtime before losing. The Lions' 4-22 record against the Vikings was the result of a cellar-dweller being beaten repeatedly by a good team. Oddly enough, despite the different paths of the two teams during those years, a surprising number of their head-to-head matches were close. Of course, the Lions usually lost.

This second dark period ended in 2011 when the Lions swept the Vikings. From 2011-22, the Lions had a 37 percent win rate in the series and swept the Vikings again in 2014 and 2016. The success rate of 37 percent isn't great but it's better than 15 percent.

Late to the Game

If any one game perhaps best illustrates the Vikings' hex over the Lions, it might be the contest that took place at the Pontiac Silverdome on September 26, 1976. It was a critical early-season game. The Lions entered with a 1-1 record while the Vikings were 1-0-1. The 2-0 Bears had first place in the Central. If the Lions won and the Bears lost, Detroit would be in a first-place tie with Chicago and a half-game ahead of Minnesota. The Lions had high expectations because they had several good players and during the previous two seasons had split the four games against the Vikings. Lions' fans were excited: over 77,000 tickets were sold. Many thought the hex was over.

The Vikings spent the night before the game at the Northfield Hilton in Troy, near the intersection of Crooks Road and I-75 which is about five miles south of where the Silverdome was located. Official game time was 1:00 PM and the Vikings' plan was to follow their standard procedure of arriving an hour early. The trip takes about ten minutes in normal traffic, but after asking around the team decided to allow an extra ten minutes. So, the team-buses left the hotel at 11:40 AM, planning to reach the stadium at noon. Afterwards, the Vikings' team spokesman said: "We always check as many people as possible and the bus company as to when we should leave our hotel. We've been doing this for 10 years and this has never happened before. I've never seen a traffic tie up like this one."[84]

The Vikings were caught in one of those infamous Silverdome traffic jams. Their team-buses crawled along the interstate along with thousands of other vehicles carrying the enormous crowd headed to the game. The ride took over an hour, and the buses pulled up to the Silverdome at 12:50 PM with kickoff scheduled for 1:07 PM. The Minnesota Vikings were late to the game.

They hurriedly dressed and then rushed to the field where they were given ten minutes to warm up. The game started twenty-two minutes late and the Vikings were assessed a delay of game penalty on the kickoff. At the outset everything seemed to be in the Lions' favor. The fans had to be thinking (as the author was):

> *The Vikings are on their heels, they haven't had enough time to get ready, they're out of their routine, the stadium is packed, and the Lions are out for blood.*
> *Surely, we'll win today!*

Minnesota fumbled the opening kickoff but, as a foreshadow of how the game would go, recovered the ball. The Lions' defense forced a punt, and then Detroit's offense moved the ball down the field. However, the drive came to an abrupt halt on the Minnesota 28-yard line when Lions' running back Horace King lost the first of his two fumbles. It turned out to be a huge mistake because the game evolved into a defensive struggle where points were at a premium. Both defenses held strong and the teams headed to the locker rooms at halftime locked in a 0-0 tie.

Vikings' quarterback Fran Tarkenton (HOF) didn't play in the second half because he'd suffered a rib injury in the second quarter when tackled by Lions' linebacker Paul Naumoff. Detroit's defense continued their solid play. They yielded just four second-half first downs, but the Vikings scored 10 points, three of them coming off King's second fumble of the day, this one on the Lions' 36-yard line. The Vikings' touchdown came in the fourth quarter when a 50-yard drive ended with a 5-yard draw play that put Vikings' running back Chuck Foreman in the end zone. The Vikings were ahead 10-3 when the Lions took possession of the ball midway through the fourth quarter. They worked the ball down the field to a first and goal on the Vikings' 1-yard line.

But four running attempts into the middle of one of pro football's best defensive lines failed, and the Vikings took over on downs. The Lions' defense forced another punt and the Lions' offense tried again, this time from the Minnesota 46-yard line.

Six plays later the Lions were back on the Minnesota 1-yard line. This time they cashed in when quarterback Greg Landry completed a pass to tight end Charlie Sanders (HOF) in the end zone. Touchdown Lions! The crowd was ecstatic. The Lions were an extra point away from tying the game.

On the PAT the snap to holder (and backup QB) Joe Reed was a good one. But the ball hit the heel of his hand and Reed bobbled it for a crucial moment. It messed-up the timing of the play and gave the Vikings' rushers time to draw near. By the time Reed spotted the ball it was too late. The extra point was blocked and the Lions were down 10-9.

"It was catchable," said Reed. "If you want to put the blame on someone, blame me…I dopped it."[85]

They had one last chance before it was over: a 57-yard field goal try for the win. But the kick failed and the hex continued.

Everything was in the Lions' favor that day. The Vikings were late to the game, the Silverdome was filled with screaming fans, and the Lions were hungry for victory. And still they couldn't beat the Vikings.

The Bears also lost that day, so the Vikings headed back to Minnesota in first place in the Central with a 2-0-1 record. The Lions were 1-2 and in third place, 1½ games behind the Vikings. The Vikings went on to post an 11-2-1 record, win the division, and advance to the Super Bowl which they lost to the Oakland Raiders. The Lions ended the season in third place with a 6-8 record.

The Lions lost six of their next seven against the Vikings.

All Too Typical

Many of the Lions' losses to Minnesota were like that one in 1976. But for a little thing here, a little thing there, the Lions might've won or at least tied. Here are a few more examples:

November 15, 1970, Bloomington, Minnesota: The 1970 season started out well for the Lions. At the end of Week 6, they were 5-1 and tied with Minnesota atop the Central Division. But things began to unravel on November 1st when the Vikings visited Tiger Stadium. They soundly defeated Detroit 30-17 in a game where Minnesota led 24-17 at halftime, and then lowered the boom by holding the Lions scoreless in the second half. A week later in New Orleans, the Lions suffered the improbable loss to the Saints when Tom Dempsey kicked his record-setting 63-yard field goal at the final gun (see Chapter 10). That loss put the Lions at 5-3, with their next game being the rematch against the 7-1 Vikings in Minnesota. If Detroit could win, they'd be just one game behind Minnesota in the standings. If they lost, they'd be three games back and needing a miracle to win the division. It was a huge game for the Lions.

As has happened so many times in Lions/Vikings games', the Lions scored first. In the first quarter, Detroit quarterback Greg Landry, making his first start of the season, threw a pass to wide receiver Larry Walton who was running into the end zone. Fighting the sun in his eyes, Walton couldn't make the catch, stumbled through the back of the end zone, and was injured when he crashed into a fence. The Lions settled for a field goal. The Vikings matched it with a field goal of their own, and on the ensuing kickoff Lions' defensive back Bobby Williams, who'd had a terrible day in the Lions' loss to the Vikings in Detroit, returned the kick 85 yards for a touchdown.

The only scoring in the second quarter came after Minnesota blocked a Detroit punt. The Vikings took possession on the Lions' 23-yard line, and moments later running back Clinton Jones scored the first of his three touchdowns of the day. The score was 10-10 at halftime.

The Lions dominated the third quarter. Their second touchdown resulted from a Vikings' turnover as Bobby Williams, still making amends for his bad game two weeks before, forced a fumble when he hit Vikings' quarterback Dr. Gary Cuozzo (a practicing dentist). Cuozzo coughed up the ball and Alex Karras (HOF) recovered it on the Vikings' 9-yard line. The Lions scored on a 5-yard pass play to Mel Farr and the extra point gave them a 17-10 lead. Later in the quarter Lem Barney (HOF) returned a punt 24 yards that set up the Lions' final score of the day, an 18-yard field goal by Errol Mann. At the end of three quarters, Detroit led 20-10.

Dr. Cuozzo warmed up in the fourth. He completed a 40-yard pass that led to Jones's second TD run of the day. It was Lions 20, Vikings 17 with ten minutes left. The Lions received the kickoff and drove down the field. A 38-yard field goal attempt by Mann failed. It was his second miss of the day.

The play of the game occurred with four minutes left. The Vikings faced third and 10 on their own 46-yard line. Detroit was in a prevent defense with six defensive backs on the field. The scheme called for double-covering the wide receivers on both edges, which left two defensive backs to cover the middle. The Vikings responded with an offensive set they rarely used, the "wide option" where running back John Lindsey lined up in the tight end position. The play called for Lindsey to run down the middle and look for a pass. After the game, Lindsey said: "I lined up on the left side. [Defensive back] Tommy Vaughn was opposite me and playing me like a linebacker would, with both hands up to hold me off."

But just before the snap, Vaughn moved away to double cover the wide receiver on the outside, which left Lindsey with single coverage down the middle. Wayne Rasmussen was the defender and Lindsey just beat him down the field. When Lindsey saw the ball coming, he thought the pass was too long and he wouldn't be able to catch it. But he did, just barely.

The catch was made at the Lions' 10-yard line and Lindsey was tackled on the 5. The Vikings scored on Clinton Jones's third running touchdown of the day. Final score: Vikings 24, Lions 20.

It was a devastating loss, the Lions' third in a row after starting the season 5-1, and it put the Vikings in command of the Central Division. But it's a testament to how good the 1970 Lions were that it didn't ruin their season. They proceeded to win their next five games, finish at 10-4, and qualify for the playoffs as the first-ever NFC wild card team.

As things turned out, if the Lions had won that game in Minnesota and everything else had been the same, the Lions and Vikings would have ended the season 11-3. The first tiebreaker was head-to-head play, and both teams would've been 1-1. The second tiebreaker was record in the conference and here the Vikings prevailed.[86] The Vikings would've won the Central Division and the playoff settings for both teams would have been just the way they turned out to be. Detroit went on the road to Dallas where they lost 0-5, while the Vikings were at home against San Francisco. Minnesota was defeated 14-17.

But what if the Lions had won that game in Minnesota and Tom Dempsey had missed the field goal attempt in New Orleans?

September 20, 1971, Detroit, Michigan: The Lions wanted to avenge their two losses to the Vikings during the 1970 season and what better way to do it than in the first game of the year, at home, on Monday Night Football? Could the setup be any better?

Monday Night Football telecasts began on ABC Television in 1970 and they were an instant hit.[87] It was Sunday afternoon football of the day on steroids: more cameras, greater use of instant replay, enhanced graphics, and three announcers in the booth instead of two. Veteran play-by-play man Keith Jackson (replaced by Frank Gifford in 1971) was teamed up with two analysts—attraction grabbers Don Meredith and Howard Cosell. Meredith was an easygoing, likeable character while Cosell was brash and controversial. The ratings were sky-high, attracting about a third of all television sets turned on during the time slot. The games were often a topic of discussion the following day at workplaces across America. In its early years, Monday Night Football was an EVENT.

The Lions' first game of 1971 was actually their third appearance on MNF. During the 1970 season they'd been on twice: at home against Chicago and on the road in Los Angeles. The Lions won both. The second game was especially thrilling: a 28-23 win before a crowd of nearly 80,000 at the LA Coliseum. As opening night of 1971 approached, the excitement level in Southeastern Michigan was high: first game, the Lions coming off a playoff year, national television, the Vikings.

But the script that is now so painfully familiar to Lions' fans played out: Lions take lead, Lions' lead dwindles, Lions lose game. This one started about as well as any Lions' fan could've hoped. Detroit opened with a drive that stalled on the Minnesota 12-yard line. Errol Mann kicked a field goal to make it 3-0. On the ensuing kickoff, the Vikings' Clinton Jones, without any help from the opposition, dropped the ball and the Lions recovered on the 22. A few plays later, Mel Farr scored on a 3-yard pass from Greg Landry. The extra point made it Lions 10, Vikings 0. Incredibly, the Vikings fumbled the next kickoff too, which the Lions recovered at the Vikings' 35. When the Lions couldn't get a first down Errol Mann tried a 40-yard field goal. It hit the crossbar: no good.

Dr. Gary Cuozzo was back to torment the Lions but his time to shine didn't begin until late in the half. In the second quarter, after Mann missed from 53, Cuozzo threw an interception which gave the Lions the ball on the Minnesota 27. The offense was stymied again and settled for a field goal. The Lions were up 13-0, but their lead could've been so much larger. Up to that point they had completely outplayed the Vikings.

The Vikings started to generate offense late in the second quarter when Cuozzo warmed up. Pass completions moved the team down the field, and they kicked a field goal with 0:03 left. The halftime score was 13-3.

The second half belonged to the Vikings. Cuozzo completed passes while Landry did not.

Cuozzo ended the night 19-32 for 232 yards, while Landry was 8-26 for 61 yards. The Vikings scored their lone touchdown on their first possession of the second half, on a 42-yard scoring play to receiver Bob Grim. Then the Vikings' defense muzzled the Lions' offense and when the Lions did get close, Errol Mann—who was one of the best NFL kickers of his era—was having a Night From Hell. He missed another 53-yard attempt, then from 36.

The Vikings kicked two more field goals, the second coming after Lem Barney fumbled a kickoff which the Vikings recovered on the Lions' 20. The Vikings led 16-13 and the clock was running out.

The Lions had one more chance. It came with less than a minute remaining when the Vikings punted to the Lions and Lem Barney was face-masked on the return. The Lions had the ball on the Vikings' 45-yard line. They moved it down to the 26 with most of the gain coming on a pass from Landry to receiver Earl McCullough. The clock was running down and the Lions were out of time-outs so Landry threw an incompletion to leave time for a field goal attempt.

The fans started booing while the Lions set up for the 33-yard field goal try. The crowd at Tiger Stadium was disappointed that the Lions had played so well in the first half and so badly in the second half. They were disappointed that the Lions would, at best, tie a game they'd had so many chances to win. Mann kicked the ball and when it sailed wide-right the boos became deafening. Mann left the field with his head in his hands; he'd made two of seven field goal attempts (although two of the misses were from 53 yards away). The final score was Vikings 16, Lions 13. It was Detroit's seventh consecutive loss to Minnesota.

November 12, 1972, Bloomington, Minnesota: The Lions arrived in Minnesota in first place and left town in second place. Once again, a special teams' failure in the final seconds cost the Lions the game.

The score was 3-0 Vikings at the end of the first half. The excitement took place in the second half. It started when Minnesota scored a touchdown and the Lions responded with two of their own, both touchdown passes from Greg Landry to Larry Walton. The Lions led 14-10 at the end of three quarters.

Minnesota took the lead back in the fourth with two field goals. The first trimmed the Lions lead to 14-13, and the second occurred after a Lions' fumble. Detroit was in their own end and Landry completed a pass to the usually sure-handed Charlie Sanders. Sanders had a first down and was struggling for more yards when he was hit from behind by the Vikings' Jeff Wright. The ball came loose and linebacker Roy Winston picked it up and ran. He was tackled on the Lions' 17. A few plays later Fred Cox kicked a 23-yarder and the Vikings led 16-14. There were four minutes left.

The Lions took the kickoff and worked their way down the field. The clock was stopped with 0:05 left when the Lions lined up for a 33-yard field goal to win. The ball was snapped, the hold was placed, and Errol Mann stepped into the ball.

"I've never been so sure about a field goal in my life," said Mann afterwards. "The moment I hit it, I knew we had the game won. I can't believe [what happened]."[88]

Mann didn't see the Vikings' Bobby Bryant charging in from the left. Bryant blocked the kick by taking it in the mouth. The ball ricocheted back toward Mann and the game was over.

In the Lions' locker room after the game, *Detroit Free Press* reporter Joe Falls approached linebacker Mike Lucci. "I don't want to hear anything about jinxes," said Lucci. "I feel like we've been six inches short for the last 10 years."[89]

September 30, 1979, Pontiac, Michigan: The 1979 season was one of the worst ever for the

Detroit Lions, and that's saying a lot. A combination of injuries and bad play got them off to a bad start and as the season dragged on the misery continued. The Lions finished in last place in the Central with a 2-14 record. The Vikings weren't tearing up the division either: they went 7-9 and ended the season in third place. Two of their seven wins came at the expense of the Lions.

The game in Pontiac was their first meeting of the year, and the Lions never led. In fact, the Lions' offense didn't cross the 50-yard line in the first half and made it there just twice in the second half. Both times they scored.

They might not have won the game, but they could've earned a tie. Playing before a crowd of over 75,000 fans at the Silverdome, the final score was Vikings 13, Lions 10. The margin of victory was a field goal Detroit handed to Minnesota at the very end of the first half. Another defensive struggle, it looked like the teams would head to the locker room at halftime in a scoreless tie. But the play of the game occurred as the clock expired at the end of the half. The Vikings completed a pass and their receiver ran out of bounds at the Lions' 37-yard line. If nothing else had happened, the half would've been over.

Unfortunately for the Lions, defensive back Luther Bradley hit the receiver out of bounds and was called for a personal foul. The penalty did two things: (1) advanced the ball to the Lions' 22-yard line, and (2) gave the Vikings one more play. The Vikings took the gift and kicked a field goal to go up 3-0.

Both teams scored ten points in the second half. But the gift field goal at the end of the first half was enough to give the Viking a 3-point victory.

December 19, 2004, Detroit, Michigan: The 2004 season was roughly the midpoint of the Matt Millen era. He'd been in charge of the team since 2001 and would keep his job until 2008. Matt Millen's tenure is the topic of Chapter 7, but those dismal days come up here because the Lions/Vikings' games of 2004 are notable enough to include in this chapter about the Minnesota hex.[90]

The Lions were having another mediocre season. They entered the game 5-8 and had lost six of their last seven games. The Vikings were 7-6 and still in the hunt for the North Division title. The December 19th game in Detroit was the second meeting of the two teams; the October 12th game in Minnesota had been yet another version of the tired movie about a Lions' team jumping to a lead and then blowing it. In that game, the Lions led 19-7 at the end of the third quarter. They lost 22-19.

The contest at Ford Field followed a different script. The Lions made the supreme effort. Three players had flu symptoms including quarterback Joey Harrington who was so sick that Head Coach Steve Mariucci didn't think he could play. But fluids were administered intravenously to Harrington before and during the game and, amazingly, he had his (up to that time) career-best day. He completed 25 of 44 passes for 361 yards. Receiver Roy Williams played through a painful hip injury. The players gave it everything they had.

Detroit opened the scoring with a field goal and then Minnesota came back to score a touchdown. In the second quarter the Vikings scored again, this time on a third-and-24 play, an 82-yard bomb from Daunte Culpepper to Randy Moss. Culpepper, a future Lion, also had a big day: 404 yards of passing and three touchdowns. Detroit responded with an 82-yard touchdown drive, and then a 23-yard field goal. The halftime score was Vikings 14, Lions 13.

The third quarter was scoreless, although Detroit had chances. They fumbled and threw an interception while in field goal range.

In the fourth quarter, both teams scored two touchdowns. The Vikings were first, and the extra point made it 21-13. Then the Lions came back, a 9-yard pass from Harrington to Williams that narrowed the Vikings' lead to 21-19. The Lions went for a two-point conversion and Harrington hit receiver Tai Streets in the end zone for two. The game was tied.

The Vikings came back with an 83-yard drive and touchdown. The extra point was successful, and they led 28-21. The clock read 1:37.

The Lions executed the hurry-up drill. It was a nine-play 80-yard drive, with most of the yardage coming on Harrington completions of 9, 7, 15, and 23 yards. Then Minnesota was called for pass interference in the end zone: it was Lions' ball, first and goal on the 1. Harrington hit Roy Williams in the left corner of the end zone for the touchdown, and the clock stopped with 0:08 left. The crowd was in a frenzy. The Lions were an extra point away from sending the game to overtime.

The long-snapper was Don Muhlbach. A rookie, Muhlbach had been signed in November to replace the injured Joey Littleton. After the signing, General Manager Matt Millen described Muhlbach as the "Nolan Ryan of long snappers."[91] Muhlbach's snap hit the ground before it reached holder Nick Harris who then struggled to get the ball in position for the kick. Before he could succeed, he was hit by a Viking and the PAT attempt failed. The Lions lost, 27-28.[92]

Not All Doom and Gloom

Given the sad litany above, readers may think the Lions have never enjoyed triumphs over the Vikings. That, of course, is not true. It's just that the Vikings have had many more triumphs over the Lions than the Lions have had over the Vikings.

Nonetheless, the Lions have enjoyed a few great moments against the Purple Gang. The Lions 20-16 win in Minnesota during the 1974 season broke a thirteen-game losing streak against the Vikings. The outcome of the game was in doubt until Lem Barney intercepted a pass in the end zone as time expired to seal the victory. In 1975, the Lions won the first-ever game against the Vikings in the Silverdome by a score of 17-10. There was a great moment in 1981 when the Lions crushed the Vikings 45-7, allowing Detroit fans to vent years of frustration in one afternoon. Or the two victories over Minnesota during 2000-2009 (the *only* two over that span), both at home and both close games. Then there were the season sweeps of the Vikings in 2014 and 2016 when the Lions were in the hunt for the North title. They came in second but reached the playoffs as wild cards.

The problem is, as inspiring as these Lions' victories over the Vikings have been, they've also been rare. In addition, many of them didn't matter in terms of helping the Lions win division titles or reach the playoffs. When the victories did matter, it was often to help the Lions become a wild card bubble team that wasn't expected to go far in the playoffs.

There have been a few exceptions, important games against Minnesota where the Lions emerged victorious. One took place in 1983, a late-season game in Pontiac that the Lions won 13-2 while marching toward their first Central Division title. Another took place in 1995 when the Lions made their improbable run to the playoffs. That was the season when the team started out 0-3, improved to 3-6, and then went on a seven-game winning streak to finish 10-6 and qualify for the playoffs as a wild card. During the late-season run they met the Vikings at the Silverdome on Thanksgiving Day and won 44-38. That Lions' team didn't look like a bubble team; instead they were on an amazing hot streak with huge momentum heading into the playoffs. Believe it or not, the Lions were favored in the playoff game against the Eagles in Philadelphia. Imagine: the Detroit Lions favored in an outdoor playoff game on the road. Would you take that bet?

There was one win over Minnesota that was the biggest of them all. It took place at the Silverdome and was the fifth game of the 1991 season. As described in Chapter 2, the 1991 season was among the Lions' best since 1957. Yet early on, fans didn't expect much, in large part because their team had done little of note since 1983. The October 6th game against Minnesota changed everything because it demonstrated that the 1991 Lions had talent and drive. They did to the Vikings what the Vikings had done to them so many times over the years: fall behind early, then stage an improbable, rousing comeback to win at the end.

The Vikings spent the first three-plus quarters building a lead. The Lions helped by shooting themselves in the foot with penalties and an interception. When Minnesota kicked a field goal to make the score 20-3 the clock showed 8:38 left in the fourth quarter. The situation looked hopeless for Detroit.

The Vikings kicked off and the Lions downed the ball in the end zone. On the first play from the 20, Barry Sanders ran left but was tacked for a loss. Quarterback Rodney Peete then threw short passes to Brett Perriman and Sanders which gave the Lions a first down on their 32. On the next play, wide receiver Robert Clark lined up on the right side and went out for a pass. He faked toward the sideline, the Viking cornerback bought it, and then Clark took off down the field between the right hashmark and sideline with the defensive back chasing behind. The Vikings' safety was too far away to make a difference. Peete threw the ball and Clark caught it on the Vikings 40-yard line and streaked to the end zone. The PAT made it Vikings 20, Lions 10. There was 6:50 left in the game.

Coach Wayne Fontes called for an onside kick. Eddie Murray kicked the ball to the left and Vikings' linebacker Greg Manusky had the best chance to grab it. But he couldn't hang on and the Lions recovered. Starting on their own 43, they rode Barry Sanders toward the end zone. Sanders handled the ball five times on the drive (four runs and one pass) and moved it to the Vikings 16-yard line. That's when Rodney Peete connected with wide receiver Willie Green in the end zone. The PAT made the score Vikings 20, Lions 17. The clock read 4:22.

The Lions kicked off to the Vikings, and the defense made a three-and-out stand. The Lions burned one time-out during the series. The Vikings punted and during the return Lions' defensive back Ray Crockett was called for an illegal block. The Lions started on their 28 with 2:55 left.

Using a combination of runs and passes, the Lions worked the ball down the field. Barry Sanders, Willie Green, and Mike Farr (Mel's son) made receptions. Sanders carried the ball four times. The big play started on the Vikings 15-yard line with 0:43 left. On third-and-1, Peete handed off to Sanders again. Sanders made one of the great runs of his amazing career, shaking-and-baking his way through the middle toward the end zone. The Vikings tackled him just as he reached the line and when his knee hit the turf, the ball was in the end zone. Touchdown Lions! The PAT made the score Lions 24, Vikings 20. The clock read 0:36.

The Vikings had the ball one last time but three pass attempts failed. When time expired the Lions had their greatest fourth-quarter comeback victory since 1957. And it tasted even better they'd done it against the Minnesota Vikings.

When the teams met again in Minnesota on November 24th the Lions won handily, 34-14, which raised their record to 8-4. It was their first season sweep of the Vikings since 1962.

Chapter 5
The Washington Jinx

Fact: The Detroit Lions have never won a football game in Washington DC.

Another team that has caused much pain for the Detroit Lions and their fans is the NFL's Washington Commanders, formerly known as the Braves, Redskins, and Washington Football Team. Since 1934, the Lions have won just 33 percent of their games against the franchise, a number so abysmal it merits discussion. When the record is examined more closely it's even worse because the Lions won the first five when the Braves/Redskins were located in Boston. If we subtract those victories the Lions' winning percentage against Washington drops to 24 percent. Three of Detroit's post-1957 playoff losses have come at the hands of Washington including the Lions' defeat in the 1991 NFC Championship Game. In addition, during the sixty years the Washington franchise played their home games in the District of Columbia the Lions managed the almost unbelievable feat of never winning a game there.

There's a jinx against the Lions when they play in Washington DC and it's never been broken. Here's the story.

Great Start, Then Disaster

Today's Washington Commanders joined the NFL in 1932 as the Boston Braves. That same year they played the Portsmouth Spartans (the future Detroit Lions) in Portsmouth, and the Spartans were victorious. The following year the Braves changed their name to Redskins and were defeated again by Portsmouth, this time in Boston.

In 1934 the Portsmouth Spartans became the Detroit Lions and beat the Boston Redskins in Detroit. During the Lions' championship year of 1935, the teams played twice with Detroit winning both games, one at home and one away. So, by the end of the 1935 season the Lions were off to a fabulous start: the Spartans/Lions had a 5-0 record against the Braves/Redskins and the domination was complete. In those five games Boston scored a total of seven points.

The Redskins were much improved in 1936. They won the Eastern Division but lost to the Packers in the NFL Championship Game. (The Lions and Redskins did not meet that season.) Yet despite their on-field success the team had trouble attracting fans in Boston and that's why they moved to Washington DC in 1937. Team owner George Preston Marshall—a showman at heart—wanted to stir up fan excitement in their new home city so he hired a team band, had them play a team fight song, and staged halftime shows.[93] Things turned out well for the team in Washington because they enjoyed several years of success and developed a loyal fan base. Their move to DC also marks the time when the Lions began losing to Washington.

From the late 1930s to mid-1940s the Lions went from a middle-of-the-pack team to the cellar (0-11 in 1942) while Washington became one of the NFL's top teams. From 1937-45, Washington played in five NFL Championship Games and won three of them. The Lions' and Redskins' divergent fortunes were on display when they met on the field: they played six times during that span—three in Detroit and three in Washington—and Washington won them all. The first time the Lions beat the Redskins after their move to DC was in 1947, a 38-21 victory in

Detroit.

That 1947 Lions' victory was one of just three during the sixty seasons (1937-1996) that the Redskins were based in the District of Columbia. During those years, the teams met twenty-eight times and the Lions' record in those games was 3-25. Eighteen of those games were played in the District of Columbia, and the Lions lost all of them. It's an astounding record of futility.

Why, Why, Why?

One reason for Detroit's dismal record against Washington was that the teams rarely played during the Lions' gravy days of the 1950s. At the time the NFL consisted of two conferences, American and National (changed to Eastern and Western in 1953). The Lions were in the six-team National (Western) Conference. Each team played a twelve-game regular season and faced conference opponents twice. In other words, ten out of the twelve regular season games were against conference rivals, leaving just two games against teams from the other conference. Since the Lions were in the West and the Redskins in the East, the likelihood of them meeting in any given season was low. For this reason, during the decade of Lions' glory (and while Washington was on the skids), the teams met just twice. Detroit won at home in 1951 and lost in Washington in 1956.

This scheduling arrangement continued until the late 1960s. The teams played twice during that decade as well, with Washington winning in 1965 (which made the Lions 0-6 in Washington) and Detroit victorious at home in 1968. The 1968 win was the Lions' last against Washington at home or away for nearly thirty years.

The 1967 NFL realignment caused Detroit and Washington to meet more often. The Western Conference was split into two four-team divisions, Central and Coastal. The Lions were in the Central and played division opponents (Chicago, Green Bay, Minnesota) twice each year and Coastal Division teams once for a total of ten games. The season had been extended to fourteen games so the Lions played four Eastern Conference teams, meaning they were more likely to draw Washington. That is exactly what happened: the teams began seeing each other every two or three years which gave the Lions more chances to lose. Following the Lion's 1968 win in Detroit the team proceeded to drop their next sixteen games against Washington. The Lions couldn't beat them at home or on the road.

We know the Lions have had some dreadful teams since the 1950s. Yet it is also true there were some quality teams. How could the Lions post such an awful record against Washington? And how could the Lions lose *every single game played in Washington DC over six decades?*

In a nutshell, it happened because when the teams began meeting more frequently Washington was one of the premier teams in football and the Lions were not. Then, on those occasions when the Lions had quality teams, Washington was better. Finally, during games when the Lions might have eked out a victory, Lions' luck reared its ugly head.

Washington Descendent

As noted earlier, Washington had a great run from the late 1930s to the mid-1940s. But then the team entered a drought that lasted until the late 1960s. A key reason for team's decline was their unwillingness to employ black players.

The NFL had been racially integrated during the 1920s and early 1930s but that changed with the Great Depression. As economic conditions worsened across the country there was a shortage of jobs and a surplus of workers. The attitude at the time was that jobs held by blacks were jobs not going to whites, so there was a move among employers to replace black workers with white workers. This mentality was widespread and it prevailed in the NFL. Washington's owner George Preston Marshall led the charge by engineering a "gentlemen's agreement" among the owners not to sign black players. As the Depression deepened, the number of black players dwindled until by the 1934 season none remained. The league remained all white until 1946.

Meanwhile, blacks were attending Northern colleges and playing football there. Some of these players were outstanding, and in 1946 when Paul Brown formed the Cleveland Browns of the new All American Football League he signed two black players: Bill Willis (HOF) and Marion Motley (HOF).[94] The NFL's Los Angeles Rams followed suit and signed Kenny Washington and Woody Strode.[95] The color line had been broken and teams knew that in order to compete with the Browns and Rams they had to sign black players too. One by one the dominoes fell and professional football reintegrated. Except for Washington that is; their owner G.P. Marshall was the last holdout, keeping the Redskins all white (how's that for irony?) until 1962.

During the first several years following reintegration, NFL teams didn't have many black players but, as would be expected in a discriminatory environment, the ones they had were outstanding. For example, the NFL Champion 1957 Detroit Lions had two non-white players: NFL Hall of Fame running back John Henry Johnson and All-Pro offensive lineman Charlie Ane.[96] The Washington franchise, by refusing to hire some of America's top football talent, placed itself at a disadvantage. Following the 1945 championship their fortunes declined and stayed low until well into the 1960s. These were the years when the Lions scored their only three victories against the Redskins while the team was based in the District of Columbia—in 1947, 1951, and 1965.

Washington's rise from the ashes began in the late 1960s. Marshall had been debilitated by a stroke back in 1963 and team control eventually passed to DC lawyer Edward Bennett Williams. In 1969, the team hired Packers' legend Vince Lombardi to coach the team. Lombardi brought attitude and improvement, but his tenure lasted only one season because he fell ill with cancer and died in 1970. George Allen—who'd had success coaching the LA Rams—was hired in 1971 and promptly signed veteran players to create a quick winner. Nicknamed the "Over the Hill Gang," the team made the playoffs in Allen's first year and then four of the next five seasons. The team played in the Super Bowl at the end of the 1972 season but lost to the perfect-season Miami Dolphins. Allen left after the 1977 season, a few lean years followed, and then in 1981 Joe Gibbs was hired to coach the team. Gibbs was the architect of the Redskins' greatest modern-day success: he served as head coach from 1981-1992 and during that time the team made the playoffs eight out of twelve seasons, played in four Super Bowls and won three of them. Lions' fans could only dream.

The Jinx

Most of the Lions' losses in the District of Columbia were thrashings by a superior team, like the 7-31 blowout in the 1982 playoffs, the crunching 0-45 regular season loss in 1991, and the 10-41 beating in the 1991 NFC Championship Game. But a few times the Lions came close, games where a break here or there could have broken the jinx. However, it never happened.

October 6, 1946, Griffith Stadium: Washington 17, Detroit 16. After scoring a touchdown late in the fourth quarter to draw within 1 point, the Lions successfully executed an onside kick. They moved the ball to Washington's 23-yard line but were stopped short on third down. With two minutes left in the game, they attempted a 30-yard field goal for the lead.[97] Lions' offensive guard and placekicker Damon Tassos missed the kick and Washington ran out the clock to secure the victory.

November 11, 1956, Griffith Stadium: Washington 18, Detroit 17. This is a game that, on paper at least, the Lions should've won. They were 9-3 that season, and missed being in the NFL Championship Game only because the Bears finished 9-2-1. Washington had a 6-6 record. The Lions had a sloppy day, throwing four interceptions and dropping several passes, yet they were down just 1 point after scoring a touchdown late in the fourth-quarter. They tried an onside kick but it failed, and Washington ran out the clock for the win. The *Detroit Free Press* called Detroit's inability to win in Washington (0-5 since 1938) a "jinx" and this was in 1956![98]

November 8, 1981, RFK Stadium: Washington 33, Detroit 31. The Lions fumbled away the opening kickoff and a few minutes later fumbled again deep in their own end. Both fumbles led to Washington scores, which put the Lions down 10-0 less than eight minutes into the game. Detroit got their act together, mounted a comeback, and took a 31-30 lead with 2:58 left in the fourth quarter. Following the kickoff, Washington drove down the field and kicked a 44-yard field goal with 43 seconds left to take a 33-31 lead. Washington kicked off to Detroit, and the Lions were able to move into position for a Hail Mary play. Quarterback Eric Hipple completed a 48-yard pass to Mark Nichols as time expired, but Nichols was tackled at the two-yard line. After the game, Hipple said: "I thought I had put it in the end zone."[99]

September 20, 1992, RFK Stadium: Washington 13, Detroit 10. This was a rematch of the 1991 NFC Championship Game. Coming off their best season in years, the Lions and their fans expected great things in 1992. The Lions saw the game as a chance for revenge against the reigning Super Bowl Champs, and an opportunity to show that the Lions were contenders again. However, the game demonstrated how badly the Lions missed offensive guards Mike Utley and Eric Andolsek. Utley had been paralyzed in November 1991 when his head hit the turf during a game in Pontiac, and Andolsek had died during the offseason when he was hit by a truck in front of his home in Louisiana. The Lions' offense managed just eight first downs, 206 yards total offense, and Barry Sanders was held to 34 yards in 14 attempts. Poor execution by the Lions' offense didn't help: Lions' receivers dropped several passes, including a sure touchdown throw mishandled by receiver Reggie Barrett. On that possession the Lions settled for a field goal. Also, two critical referee calls went against the Lions. The defense played well, holding Washington to 13 points but it wasn't enough. Detroit had a chance to tie the game with 1:42 left in the fourth quarter when rookie kicker Jason Hanson attempted a 49-yard field goal. The kick missed badly and after the game Hanson said his foot hit the ground before the ball: "I guess you could say I choked."[100]

October 22, 1995, RFK Stadium: Washington 36, Detroit 30, OT. This was the Lions' last chance to break the jinx because the Redskins moved to Landover, Maryland two years later. Another what-might-have-been game, the Lions were doomed by three fumbles and an interception. Quarterback Scott Mitchell completed 30 of 50 passes for 327 yards, but fumbled twice and both led to Washington touchdowns. Despite those errors, the Lions held a 3-point lead late in the game. Following the Lions' final punt, Washington drove from their own 20-yard line to the Lions' 22 where kicker (and former Lion) Eddie Murray made a field goal to tie the game with 0:04 left. Washington won the overtime coin flip and elected to receive. They worked the ball to the Lions' 41 but were forced to punt. The kick was downed on the Lions' 4-yard line and on the next play QB Mitchell threw an errant pass into the hands of Washington's "Ageless Wonder," cornerback Darrel Green (HOF). Green ran 7 yards to the end zone to win the game. The Jinx of Washington DC lived on.

Dan Snyder Saves the Day

The Washington Football Team moved to Landover, Maryland in 1997, and were bought by Dan Snyder two years later. The team's fans haven't been happy with Snyder because under his leadership the team has gone from being one of the NFL's premier franchises to a losing team.

Snyder has spent millions on free agents who didn't meet expectations, and changed coaches even more often than the Lions. During the twenty-three years he's owned the franchise, Washington has had ten head coaches. One of them was Joe Gibbs, the man who led the 1981-1992 Redskins juggernaut, but even he couldn't bring back the magic. Snyder has also alienated fans by raising ticket prices, suing season ticket holders, and charging fans extra to tailgate. Under his ownership the Washington Commanders (their new name as of 2022) have won 42 percent of their games.

This turmoil has been good for the Lions. Amazingly, Detroit has a 7-5 record against the Snyder-owned team. They did something else notable: they won a road game against Washington, their first since defeating the Boston Redskins in Boston in 1935. The breakout win occurred on September 22, 2013, in Landover, Maryland, with the Lions gaining a 27-20 victory. The other Lions' wins against Washington since 1997 were in Pontiac and Detroit.

So, the Lions sort-of, kind-of, broke the jinx although strictly speaking they did not. They won a road game against a team named for Washington DC, but they still haven't won a football game in the District of Columbia.

In recent years, Dan Snyder has been making noise about moving the team back to Washington. Lions' fans might prefer it remains in Maryland.

Chapter 6
Dome Sweet Dome or Dome Bad Home?

Detroit's Tiger Stadium was a wonderful place to watch a baseball game. Its short outfields and narrow foul territory made it a hitters' park and put spectators near the action. The playing field was surrounded by grandstands which held in the noise and allowed fans—especially those seated between first and third base—to hear the sounds of the game: bats meeting balls; the slap of balls on gloves; umpires calling balls and strikes; players shouting at each other. The atmosphere could be electric.

Tiger Stadium also had its drawbacks. The major flaw was thousands of seats located behind steel posts that supported the upper deck and its roof. Veteran fans knew to avoid these obstructed-view seats if possible. Another problem was bad sight lines for spectators in the lower-deck outfield seats. They viewed the game through a fence and, with the upper deck above them, had difficulty seeing fly balls.

Despite these shortcomings, Tiger Stadium was a beloved baseball venue that served Detroit's fans for nearly ninety years. Many had fond memories of the ballpark, and some openly wept when the Tigers played their final game there on September 27, 1999.

Tiger Stadium is remembered less fondly as a football venue. The basic problem was that the field and grandstands were configured for baseball, so no matter where the football field was marked out many seats were far from the action and those that were close were near the end zones. Then there were those support posts obstructing the views of baseball and football fans alike. And being an outdoor stadium, fans were sometimes uncomfortably cold at late seasons games. No one remembers anyone shedding tears when the Lions played their last game there on Thanksgiving Day 1974.

In the NFL's early days, it was common practice to play football in baseball stadiums. Unlike college football, NFL teams didn't have the fan support and revenue necessary to build their own stadiums. Instead, they did the next best thing which in many cases was to lease the local baseball stadium and play games there. In cities like Detroit with both major league baseball and football, the football team was second fiddle to the baseball team. In fact, for marketing purposes many early NFL teams tried to ride the coattails of the local baseball team by adopting the same name: the Pittsburgh Pirates, Brooklyn Dodgers, New York Yankees, New York Giants, Boston Braves, and Cincinnati Reds were all NFL teams. In other cities the football team tried to associate itself with the baseball team by using a similar name—the Detroit Lions (Tigers) and Chicago Bears (Cubs) being examples.

Professional football's fortunes began to improve in the late 1930s. Rule changes such as moving the goal posts to the goal line and allowing forward passes anywhere behind the line of scrimmage favored the offense. There was more scoring which brought in additional fans. Radio coverage expanded. Then after World War II the NFL rode the nationwide boom in spectator sports. Television coverage began in the late 1940s, then increased enormously during the 1950s and 1960s. Crowds grew bigger and money flowed in. The improvement was so profound that by the mid-1960s several cities (e.g., Pittsburgh, Atlanta, St. Louis, Philadelphia) acknowledged professional football's higher status by building multipurpose stadiums designed for both baseball and football. Kansas City went a step further by building separate baseball and football stadiums.

Meanwhile, the Lions were playing at Tiger Stadium. Lions' owner Bill Ford wanted a better venue, one with about 70,000 seats, unobstructed sight-lines, and a covered roof if possible. In true NFL style he expected someone else to pay for it.

Discussions about a new stadium had, in fact, been going on in Detroit since the 1940s. However, for several reasons—the most important being location and money—no decision had been reached.[101] By the late 1960s Ford had become impatient, in part because he saw a large segment of the Lions' fanbase leaving the city for the suburbs, especially after the 1967 Riots. He began entertaining stadium offers from suburban cities.

The City of Pontiac won the prize by luring the Lions out of Detroit with an agreement to build a domed football stadium. The preliminary deal was announced in October 1970 and finalized four months later. It called for a covered stadium with close-in parking at a cost of $41 million.[102] The City of Pontiac and the Pontiac Stadium Building Authority issued bonds to fund the project and construction began in September 1972.

The Pontiac Silverdome

Pontiac Metropolitan Stadium was the official name of the structure that became better known as the Pontiac Silverdome. Its seating capacity of just over 80,000 made it the largest indoor stadium in the world at the time, and there were several pluses for fans: grandstands close to the field, outstanding sight lines, a steep-pitched upper deck that put spectators on top of the game, and a roof to protect them from inclement weather. The original plan called for a hard-roof, but construction went over budget so a less expensive covering was used. A series of Teflon-coated panels were attached to a cable grid and the assembly was lifted into position and held there by powerful blowers that raised the air pressure inside the building to a level higher than the pressure outdoors. Entering and leaving the building was an odd experience: going in the doors meant fighting a headwind and exiting was like being squeezed out of a toothpaste tube. The name Silverdome caught on because the roof's fiberglass panels looked silver in the sunlight and, since the Lions' colors are silver and blue, it seemed like a good name for the team's new home.

The final cost of the project was $55.7 million and it opened in August 1975. Lions' fans were excited: over 50,000 season tickets were sold before the first game was played. For better or worse, a new era of Lions' football was about to begin.

Opening Night Fiasco

The Lions first regular-season game in the Silverdome took place against the Dallas Cowboys on the evening of Monday October 6, 1975. In hindsight, it wasn't the best idea to schedule a night game for the opener but everyone expected things to go smoothly because they had during two home preseason games, the first of which drew a crowd of over 60,000.[103]

Opening night was a bad scene both on and off the field. On the field, the Lions were crushed 10-36 by the Cowboys. The Lions took a 10-9 lead in the third quarter but then things fell apart. Lions' punter Herman Weaver bobbled a low snap and tried to run for the first down. He was tackled short of the marker, the Cowboys took possession, and moments later the rout was on. Dallas scored a touchdown in the third quarter and three more in the fourth quarter. Lions' quarterback Greg Landry was sacked eleven times.

The bigger story occurred off the field: monumental traffic jams both before and after the game. Traffic problems turned out to be the Silverdome's Achilles heel; the stadium, located near the intersection of the I-75 and M-59 freeways, was accessible from just a few roads. Furthermore, close-in parking concentrates automobiles and with nearly 80,000 fans in attendance there were a lot of cars to move in and out. Pregame traffic caused about 4,000 fans to miss the opening kickoff and the postgame tie-up was even worse. Drivers were confused in the dark and alcohol played a role. More booze is consumed at night games than at day games, and impaired drivers are believed to be a major reason why it took about ninety minutes to clear the Silverdome's parking lots. Since the game ended after midnight some fans weren't even out of the parking lot until nearly 2:00 AM, and then were stuck in traffic on the roads. There were reports of people arriving home at around 4:00 AM. The entire affair was a public relations disaster and earned the Silverdome a well-deserved reputation for traffic problems that plagued the facility its entire life. The traffic jams, along with the Lions defeat, made an inauspicious beginning for a stadium that would eventually bear the nicknames "Drunk Dome" and "Loser Dome."[104]

Opening night also pointed toward another of the stadium's problems: its enormous seating capacity. During the years the Lions played there the NFL had a blackout rule which prevented games from being televised locally unless the game was declared a sellout seventy-two hours prior to kickoff.[105] The opening game didn't sell out but was shown locally because the NFL issued an exemption to allow it. During much of the Silverdome's life as the Lions' home field the stadium's size, combined with the Lions' mostly poor-to-mediocre seasons while playing there, meant that Lions' home games rarely sold out. Thus, few homes games were shown on local television and based on that consideration alone Lions' fans might have been better off if their team had played in a smaller stadium.

Dome Football

Prior to the 1975 season indoor football was a rarity. The Houston Oilers (today's Tennessee Titans) had been playing in the Astrodome since 1968, but that was it for NFL dome football. Then, in 1975, the Lions moved into the Silverdome and the New Orleans Saints occupied the Superdome. The following year the Seattle Seahawks were formed and began play in the Kingdome. Since then a slow march has taken place indoors to where today about one-third of NFL teams play on a covered field.[106]

The obvious difference between indoor and outdoor football is the weather. Inside a dome the temperature is moderate, the field and ball are dry, and there's no wind to influence passes or kicks. The players and fans are removed from the elements which generally makes for a more pleasant experience. This is the case in retractable roof stadiums as well because the roof is opened on moderate, dry days and closed against unpleasant weather.

Indoor and outdoor stadium playing surfaces can differ as well. Outdoor stadiums use natural grass or artificial turf, while most covered stadiums have artificial turf.[107] Artificial grass surfaces—especially those used in the 1960s, 1970s, and 1980s—are harder than natural grass fields which allows players to run faster but also result in more injuries because hard surfaces have less give when knees, elbows, hips, and heads meet the ground.[108] In addition, the firmer footing on artificial turf means players' feet are less likely to move when their legs are hit which causes more knee and ankle injuries. Modern softer surfaces like FieldTurf have lessened these problems somewhat but the higher injury rate on artificial turf is still a major issue. Back in the Silverdome's day it was a huge issue because the stadium was known for having the hardest, fastest surface in the NFL, one that Barry Sanders describes as "basically pavement covered by a thin green rug."[109] Injuries were a special problem there, the most famous victim being Lions' offensive lineman Mike Utley. The NFL Players Association has called artificial turf an "abomination" and advocated its elimination for years.[110]

Another aspect of dome football has been the general lack of success of teams that play indoor home games. As noted earlier, NFL dome football began in 1968 and it took thirty-one years for a dome team (the 1998 Atlanta Falcons) to reach the Super Bowl. As of the 2021 season, nine dome teams have played in Super Bowls and won four Lombardi Trophies. Since the Super Bowl era began (the 1966 season) there have been fifty-seven Super Bowls involving 114 teams, so the nine dome-teams represent 8.0 percent of participants. Given the number of NFL dome teams during that period, had they been of equal quality to outdoor teams and the law of averages prevailed, we would expect them to account for around 15-20 percent of Super Bowl teams. For the NFC we would expect a larger number because most dome teams reside in that conference. Of the NFC's Super Bowl representatives, 12.5 percent have been dome teams yet the proportion of indoor teams in the conference has been much higher than that. Since 1975, the NFC has had anywhere from two to seven dome teams each season out of a total of thirteen to sixteen teams in the conference (actual numbers depend on the particular season).

Bad Teams' Homes or Domes Bad Homes?

The evidence shows that dome teams have been less successful than outdoor teams in reaching and winning Super Bowls. Has this occurred because second-tier NFL teams *chose to play in domes*? Or are dome teams less successful *because they play in domes*? Or are both factors at work?

The identities of the early dome teams suggest that less successful teams did, in fact, choose to play indoors. The first three dome teams—Houston Oilers, Detroit Lions, and New Orleans Saints—aren't on anyone's list of Dynasty Teams During the Super Bowl Era. The Oilers were a charter team of the American Football League (AFL, founded in 1960), and as an outdoor team played in the first three AFL Championship Games and won the first two. They moved indoors in 1968 and following the AFL/NFL merger (1970) had their best success in the late 1970s when they played in (and lost) two AFC Championship Games. The Lions were a dominant team in the 1950s but had just one additional playoff appearance on their resume when they moved to the Silverdome in 1975. The Saints were a 1967 expansion team and league doormat before occupying the Superdome. They stayed near the bottom of the league for years and finally made the playoffs in the 1987 season. The Seattle Seahawks were the fourth team to occupy a domed stadium. An expansion team in 1976, they called the Kingdome home for over two decades.

Thus, by the 1976 season four teams, or 14 percent of the league, were playing in domes. None of the four were considered among the NFL's elite winning teams when they moved indoors.

A glaring exception was the fifth indoor team: the Minnesota Vikings. They began play in the Metrodome in 1982 following several consecutive seasons of success earned while playing at a baseball stadium in Bloomington, Minnesota. Perennial NFC Central Division champs during the 1970s, the Vikings played in four Super Bowls from 1970-1977. They weren't a second-tier team choosing to play in a dome, they were a top-tier team that moved indoors and have accomplished somewhat less since then. As a dome team the Vikings have been in the playoffs many times and played in five NFC Championship Games but have yet to return to the Super Bowl.

Another way to examine the indoor-outdoor football issue is to look at the NFL's most successful teams. Here is the list of teams with five or more Super Bowl appearances (through 2022) along with the season they last appeared:

TEAM	NUMBER OF SBS	LAST APPEARANCE (SEASON)
New England Patriots	11	2018
Denver Broncos	8	2015
Pittsburgh Steelers	8	2010
Dallas Cowboys	8	1995
San Francisco Forty-Niners	7	2019
LA/St. Louis/LA Rams	5	2021
New York Giants	5	2011
Green Bay Packers	5	2010
Oakland/LA/Oakland/LV Raiders	5	2002
Washington Commanders	5	1991
Miami Dolphins	5	1984

Only three teams on the list have played indoor home games: the Dallas Cowboys, Las Vegas Raiders, and Los Angeles Rams. Dallas moved into their retractable roof stadium in 2009 and the Raiders became an indoor team when they moved to Las Vegas in 2020. Both teams went indoors *after* their last Super Bowl appearance. The Rams played in two Super Bowls while based in a domed stadium in St. Louis, and their 2021 appearance was at the end of their first season in Sofi Stadium in Inglewood, California. This means that every Super Bowl appearance on this list, save three by the Rams, was by a team that played their home games outdoors.

The evidence is clear: top-tier NFL teams tend to play in outdoor stadiums, and indoor teams are more likely to occupy the league's second tier. In fact, the comparison isn't close. This does not mean that all dome teams have been unsuccessful: the Rams, Colts, Falcons, Cardinals, and Saints have appeared in Super Bowls as indoor teams, with the Rams, Colts, and Saints winning Lombardi Trophies.[11] Dome teams do reach the Super Bowl and occasionally win, but it hasn't happened as often as their numbers in the league would suggest. Part of the reason why is that less successful teams have chosen to play indoors and more successful teams have chosen to stay outdoors.

Meanwhile, it is also true that playing indoors makes a team less successful. The reason why is that, generally speaking, outdoor teams do better on the road than indoor teams do. This result is most apparent in the playoffs, especially late-round playoff games. As the playoffs progress and the pyramid narrows, teams' flaws become more exposed. Indoor teams seem to have difficulty with the outdoor elements of cold, wet, and wind, all of which can be issues in January playoff games, especially in the North.

Estimates covering the 2007-19 seasons report a home-field advantage for outdoor teams playing outdoor teams of 2.29 points (i.e., outdoor home teams playing at home defeated visiting outdoor-based teams by an average of 2.29 points), but the home-field advantage for outdoor teams playing indoor teams was higher, at 2.64 points.[112] During playoff games the margin was much greater: when dome teams played on the road against outdoor teams, dome teams lost by an average of 11.31 points. *SportsInsights* reports that in playoff games over the 2003-19 seasons, outdoor teams on the road won 47.2 percent of their games against other outdoor teams while dome teams on the road managed to win only 25.0 percent of games against outdoor teams. This is not to say that dome teams can't win outdoor playoff games, just that it rarely happens. In fact, it has *never* happened in a Conference Championship Game.[113]

NFC and AFC Conference Championship games are played at the stadiums of the top-seeded team and are the final step to the Super Bowl. Dome teams have appeared in twenty-three of these games, two of which involved dome teams playing dome teams. The other twenty-one games pitted indoor teams against outdoor teams; here are the numbers:

Dome Teams *at Home* vs Outdoor Teams
Dome Teams: 7 wins, 2 losses

Dome Teams *on Road* vs Outdoor Teams
Dome Teams: 0 wins, 13 losses

The 78 percent win rate for dome teams at home is slightly higher than the 69 percent winning record for home teams in all Conference Championship Games. The road-team winning percentage in all Championship Games is 31 percent, but when a dome team is involved the number drops to 0. This difference is both sizeable and stunning. Clearly, dome teams have trouble winning outdoors, especially in January when the pressure is at its highest and the weather is most likely to be intemperate.

So, what's the answer? Are domes bad teams' homes? Or are domes bad homes? They're both.

The Lions' Experience

Dome teams have trouble winning outdoor games. Lions' fans know this because over the years they've watched their team lose outdoor road games again and again, at a much higher rate than they lose indoor home games. NFL teams typically win fewer games on the road than at home, but at times the Lions have been in a class by themselves. Many fans recall the horrid stretches from 2001-03 when they lost 24 consecutive road games, and then beat that record by losing 26 straight road games from 2007-10.

In an effort to determine the impact of the Lions' move indoors on their win/loss columns, we consider the team's home and away records during their times as outdoor and indoor teams. When the Lions arrived in Detroit in 1934, they played at the University of Detroit's stadium. The move to Tiger Stadium (named Briggs Stadium at the time) occurred in 1938 and the team stayed there through the 1974 season.[114] Every game the Lions played during those years was outdoors except one—a game in 1971 against the Oilers in Houston (which the Lions lost). The Lions played at the Silverdome from 1975-2001, then moved to Ford Field (which is also covered) in 2002. Using 1938 as the starting point, here are the Detroit Lions' win/loss records at home and away over three separate periods:

SEASONS	HOME STADIUM	WIN% AT HOME	WIN% ON ROAD
1938-1974	Tiger Stadium	54%	41%
1975-2001	Pontiac Silverdome	55%	30%
2002-2021	Ford Field	43%	27%

Two things stand out here: (1) the Lions' home winning percentage at the Silverdome is very similar to their win rate at Tiger Stadium, and (2) the road records while the team was based at the two stadiums are much different. The Lions were considerably more successful on the road as an outdoor team than as an indoor team which tells us that the Lions' diminished success after leaving Tiger Stadium came from losing more road games, not home games.

How many games did the move indoors cost the Lions? The decline in road-winning percentage from 41 percent to 30 percent over a sixteen-game schedule works out to an additional road loss of 0.9 of a game. In other words, leaving Tiger Stadium for the Silverdome appears to have cost the Lions approximately one additional road-game loss per season. That's a significant number when you realize that many seasons have ended with the Lions one victory short of being in the playoffs.

The Lions left the Silverdome for Ford Field in 2002. The Silverdome had become economically obsolete, in part because it was short on luxury boxes. In addition, the stadium's owner, the City of Pontiac, was in poor fiscal shape (partly due to losses incurred on the Silverdome) and unable to keep the structure current. By the mid-1990s the Lions wanted out and began negotiating to buy out their Silverdome lease and build a new covered stadium in Detroit. After considerable haggling with the various parties involved, the decision was made to leave Pontiac and build Ford Field at a cost of $500 million, with 51 percent of the amount paid by the City of Detroit and the remaining 49 percent borne by the Lions. Construction began in November 1999. The Lions left the Silverdome with a whimper, accumulating a 2-14 record in 2001 which was their final season in the building.

The fresh beginning at the new stadium was not a panacea. During the team's tenure at Ford Field they have been particularly inept, suffering a significant drop in performance both at home and on the road (Lions' General Manager Matt Millen had a lot to do with that—see Chapter 7). It's interesting to note that the greater decline in performance compared to their time at the Silverdome has come at home with the winning percentage 12 percentage points lower. Compared to their time at Tiger Stadium, however, the larger drop in performance as a Ford Field-based team came on the road. The Ford Field home winning percentage is 11 percent points below the number at Tiger Stadium, but the road winning percentage is 14 percentage points lower.[115]

Lest you think the results presented here are peculiar to the Lions, consider the numbers for a team similar to the Lions in a few important ways. The Minnesota Vikings are based in the North, had many outdoor-seasons (twenty-one) under their belt before they moved into a domed stadium, and made the move at roughly the same time (1982) as the Lions (1975). The Vikings have remained indoors except for a two-year stint (2014-2015) when they played home games at the University of Minnesota's outdoor stadium while waiting for US Bank Stadium to be completed. Through 2022, the Vikings have played twenty-three seasons outdoors, and thirty-nine seasons indoors. Here are their home and away records as outdoor and indoor teams:

Vikings as *Outdoor* Team

1961-1981 at Metropolitan Stadium & 2014-2015 at TCF Bank Stadium
Winning percentage at home: 63%
Winning percentage on road: 51%

Vikings as *Indoor* Team

1982-2013 at Metrodome & 2016-2022 at US Bank Stadium
Winning percentage at home: 65%
Winning percentage on road: 40%

The Vikings have been a demonstrably better team than the Lions because their home and road winning percentages are several percentage points higher than the Lions. The striking similarity between the two teams is the decline in road game-winning percentage after moving indoors. The Vikings suffered a drop of 11 percentage points which is identical to what the Lions experienced when they went from Tiger Stadium to the Silverdome. Becoming an indoor team didn't cost the Vikings at home, it cost them on the road just like it did the Lions.

What's the Problem?

The conventional wisdom in the NFL is that indoor teams don't handle outdoor elements—heat, cold, humidity, wet, wind—as well as outdoor teams. This explanation makes sense and likely results from significantly greater *game experience* (as opposed to practice experience) outdoor teams get while playing outdoors. This point is especially relevant on offense where keys to success are timing between passer and receiver, catching and holding onto the ball, and accurate placekicking. Bad weather is an impediment to offensive success, and the more game experience a team has in dealing with outdoor elements, the more likely they are to have positive results while playing in them.

The NFL's scheduling system plays an important role. Let's illustrate using the sixteen-game season that was in place from 1978-2020. A dome team like the Lions plays eight indoor home games a year. In addition, they have an indoor road game against divisional opponent Minnesota, and then typically another two or more indoor road games depending on that season's opponents. Let's suppose the Lions play three indoor road games. This means the Lions play eleven indoor games (eight at home, three away) and five outdoor road games. In terms of *game experience*, that's 69 percent indoors, 31 percent outdoors.

What about an outdoor team? The Green Bay Packers play both the Lions and Vikings on the road each year, so they're guaranteed two dome games. Then, if they get two more indoor games (again, depending on that year's schedule), that's a total of four. So, the Packers play twelve outdoor games (eight at home, four on the road) and four indoor road games. In terms of game experience, that's 75 percent outdoors, 25 percent indoors. Thus, the Packers spend considerably more of their game time outdoors than the Lions do. If experience matters in life, and most of us would agree that it does, and if the Packers and Lions are equal in all other ways (that's never true, but stay with me here), then the Packers should be a better outdoor team than the Lions and the Lions should be better indoors than the Packers.

At first glance, this indoor/outdoor split shouldn't matter to the two teams' relative win/loss records. If both teams play "better" in the environment where they play most of their games and "worse" where they play the smaller number of games, then it should roughly cancel out. In other words, one team should not accumulate a higher win/loss record than the other team based on which team plays home games indoors and which team plays home games outdoors.

But it does matter. The data provide convincing evidence that indoor teams are less successful than outdoor teams, in large part because indoor-based teams have trouble winning outdoor road games. What's going on here?

A key piece of information is that more points are scored during indoor games than outdoor games. The difference tends to be about 5 points per game.[116] This is no surprise to football fans; they know that passing games and placekicking work better indoors than outdoors. They know that adverse weather hinders offensive performance.

Here's the problem facing dome teams: they're at a disadvantage playing outdoors because they have less game experience dealing with the elements than their outdoor-based opponents. Thus, we see the reduction in road winning percentage that the Lions and Vikings experienced when they moved indoors. Notice that there was not a corresponding increase in home winning percentages. Why not? Because inside a dome their outdoor-based opponents don't have to deal with the weather either. Outdoor-based teams are perfectly capable of dealing with the indoor environment. Thus, neither team is placed at a disadvantage indoors, but the indoor team is at a disadvantage outdoors, especially late in the season when weather conditions are more likely to be poor.

Consider an analogy. Suppose we have two drivers. One grew up in Michigan and has spent years driving on dry highways, wet highways, and roads covered in snow. The second driver grew up in Florida and has extensive experience driving on dry and wet roads, but almost no experience on snow (many Floridians have never driven on snow). Snow on the roads hinders driving performance, and the Michigan driver has much more experience doing it in "game situations" than the Florida driver.

Put the Michigan driver in Florida. Is the Michigander at any disadvantage driving on Florida highways apart from being unfamiliar with particular roads? No, because the Michigander isn't likely to experience road conditions they haven't encountered many times before in Michigan. Now put the Florida driver in Michigan. Is that person at a disadvantage? Yes, if they encounter a snowstorm. Would driving a car in snow impact their performance more than it would the experienced winter driver from Michigan? The answer, of course, is yes.

This asymmetry is similar to what the dome team faces. Like the Florida driver in the Michigan snowstorm, the indoor team is at a disadvantage playing outdoors because they have less "game experience" in that environment. The outdoor team is the Michigan driver. This driver is fine driving in Florida, like the outdoor team is fine playing indoors. Thus, the indoor team is at a disadvantage outdoors, but the outdoor team is not at a disadvantage indoors. That's the problem for dome teams and it shows up most in playoff games when the pressure is at its highest and weather most likely to be an issue.

What's a Team to Do?

The results presented here suggest that the Detroit Lions gave up an advantage when they relocated indoors. It wasn't a move to dome sweet dome, it was a move to dome bad home. Another implication is that Northern teams like the Green Bay Packers, Chicago Bears, Buffalo Bills, New England Patriots, etc., should stay outdoors. Keeping fans and players comfortable inside a dome has advantages, but it comes at a cost in terms of on-field performance. The results also suggest that, if reaching the Super Bowl is the prime objective, teams that play in retractable-roof stadiums should open the roof—especially when the weather is foul—so their players acquire more outdoor-game experience. Keep the roof closed for the tractor pulls and

WrestleMania, but open it for football games.

Nothing being said here is claiming the Detroit Lions' on-field problems since 1957 are primarily due to playing indoors. That would be an absurd thing to say because there's much more influencing a team's success than whether they play indoors or outdoors. But it is safe to say that the move indoors placed the Lions at a disadvantage compared to some of their opponents and helps explain their abysmal playoff record over the last several decades. Lions fans know their team is 1-12 in playoff games since the last championship in 1957. The discussion here suggests that home field advantage in the playoffs is critically important to a dome team. The Lions have had home field advantage in just two playoff games since 1957. The Lions' lone playoff victory came in the Silverdome during the 1991 season. For the twelve losses, one was at home, eleven were on the road, two of which were in domes. So, in playoff games since 1957, the Lions are 1-1 indoors at home, 1-3 indoors at home and away, and 0-9 in outdoor road games.[117] Do these numbers make a little more sense now?

What should the Lions do? Remove Ford Field's roof? Or exit the building and move across the street to Comerica Park and share a baseball stadium with the Tigers, just like the old days? Neither of these things are going to happen but either of them would increase the Lions' probability of on-field success. The obvious disadvantage for fans would be sitting through some miserable weather while watching games. But if Bears' and Packers' fans can do it, then so can Lions' fans.[118]

What Does the Future Hold?

The move within the NFL has been toward indoor stadiums and the reason is primarily economic. Covered stadiums have the advantage that they can host events throughout the year. Conventions, circuses, basketball games, tractor pulls, auto auctions, rodeos...all of these and more have taken place in domed stadiums.[119] These events could be done outdoors but typically aren't because, unlike football games, most of them won't take place in foul weather. Meanwhile, the trend has been to build ever-grander, ever-more expensive stadiums, the most recent being the $5 billion Sofi Stadium in Englewood, California that is the new home of the Rams and Chargers. It has a covered roof but the sides are open to the weather, so it's a covered stadium that's not an indoor stadium. That distinction isn't as great in Southern California as it would be in, say, Detroit, Michigan.

If the NFL continues to move indoors and if you accept the arguments presented here, then the advantage of being an outdoor team will increase. As more teams go indoors the outdoor-game experience reaped by outdoor-based teams will become ever more valuable. Yes, outdoor teams will play more indoor games because they will have more indoor road games. But indoor-based teams will play an ever-smaller number of outdoor games each season which means that, proportionately speaking, the outdoor teams' outdoor experience will become even larger compared to indoor teams' outdoor experience.

To see why, suppose that every NFL team goes indoors except for one lone holdout. In a sixteen-game regular season format the outdoor-team holdout would play eight outdoor games and eight indoor games per season, so their indoor/outdoor split would be 50/50. Meanwhile, indoor teams would play *at most* one outdoor game a year, or 6 percent of their game experience. The other 94 percent would be indoors. Many teams would have no outdoor game experience at all. Thus, the gap between outdoor and indoor game experience for the two types of teams would be even greater than it is today. If the lone outdoor team can gain home field advantage in the playoffs they'd be even more likely to reach the Super Bowl than they are now.

Memo to Green Bay Packers' fans: make sure your team never, ever, builds a domed stadium.

Chapter 7
The Matt Millen Era

"In all my years of playing, I've never seen a year like this. It's unbelievable. I've never seen so many ways of losing. It's like we find a new way to do it every week. I don't know what to think. It's incredible."

—Lions' offensive guard Damien Woody, talking to reporters on November 21, 2004, after the Lions had blown a 19-7 fourth-quarter lead and lost to the Vikings 19-22.[120]

Even the most die-hard Lions' fans questioned their allegiance to the team during the Matt Millen Era. From January 2001-September 2008, while Matt Millen was President and CEO of the Detroit Lions, the team won 27 percent of their games. There is no other similar length of time in Lions' history when the team fared that badly, not even the grim days of 1942-1948 when the win rate was 31 percent. Over seven-plus seasons, Matt Millen hired and fired players, coaches, and front office staff while the Lions displayed enormous ineptitude on the field. Four head coaches, about sixty assistant coaches, and many more players were part of the dismal scene. Damien Woody, who in 2004 signed a lucrative free agent contract with Detroit after earning two Super Bowl rings playing for the New England Patriots, said, "I went from the mountain top to the valley low."[121]

Placing Matt Millen in charge of the Lions was an outside-the-box experiment thought up by William Clay Ford Jr (Bill Jr), son of Lions' owner William Clay Ford Sr (Bill Sr). The plan was widely hailed at the start but soon turned into a complete disaster. Matt Millen is acknowledged to have many wonderful attributes: great football player; knowledgeable of the game; honest; charismatic; intelligent; articulate. But his career track—NFL player to TV & radio football analyst to president and CEO of the Detroit Lions—went awry in its final leg. He'd been a huge success at the first two jobs, but failed miserably as an NFL team executive. The crux of the problem was poor player acquisition: bad draft picks and bad free agency signings led to bad play on the field. It was exacerbated by Millen's hiring and firing of personnel at all levels of the organization which meant there was almost no continuity. This mismanagement went on for over seven seasons and caused the team to perform so badly that the fans eventually revolted. Millen was finally fired three games into the 2008 season, but no quick turnaround resulted. Instead, inertia from years of incompetent management caused the Lions to flail away and accomplish something no other NFL team had ever done before: end their season 0-16.

Why Matt Millen?

By the late 1990s, the Bill Fords (owner Bill Sr and son Bill Jr) had decided the Lions were stuck in a rut. On one level, the team had been successful. Over the nine-year span from 1991-99, the Lions reached the playoffs six times which by that measure was the Lions' best decade ever. But there had been just the one playoff win in 1991:

<u>**Detroit Lions 1990s Playoff Appearances**</u>
1991: Lions defeat Dallas 38-6; lose to Washington 10-41
1993: Lions lose to Green Bay 24-28
1994: Lions lose to Green Bay 12-16
1995: Lions lose to Philadelphia 37-58
1997: Lions lose to Tampa Bay 10-20
1999: Lions lose to Washington 13-27

The 1991 team was loaded with talent, but within a few years many of the top players were gone. Barry Sanders continued to offer thrills but he couldn't carry the team on his back. Coach Wayne Fontes, who was fired at the end of the 1996 season, had been a "players' coach" who some observers considered too loose with his charges. This is why Bobby Ross was hired in 1997. Known as a disciplinarian, Ross enjoyed success in the college ranks before leading the 1994 San Diego Chargers to the Super Bowl. For the first time since Don McCafferty the Lions had a proven Super Bowl coach.

Bobby Ross lasted three seasons and part of a fourth. His 1997 team went 9-7 and made the playoffs, but exited after losing at Tampa Bay. That season was notable for being Barry Sanders' best ever in terms of yards gained. Sanders gained 2,053 yards in 335 rushing attempts (an incredible 6.1 yards per carry), making him just the third player to rush for over 2,000 yards in a season.[122] He also caught 33 passes for 305 yards which means he accounted for 2,358 yards of total offense. It was one of the greatest NFL seasons ever for an offensive player and earned him the league's Most Valuable Player Award.

Sanders played one more season, then retired just before the start of training camp in 1999. Later admitting his timing could've been better, he'd grown tired of the game. In his 2003 autobiography *Barry Sanders: Now You See Him,* he's very candid about why he retired.[123] He started out with the Lions during a rebuilding program in the late 1980s, played for a great team in 1991, then watched valued teammates depart which he blames on Lions' management. The team stagnated, and by the end of the 1990s another rebuilding program was in the cards. Sanders wanted to play for a winner, not go through another rebuild. He also felt that he and his teammates had done everything they could to win, but management hadn't matched the effort.

Sanders announced his retirement on July 27, 1999, and offers this take on what followed: "Part of me wants to believe that my leaving helped the organization, forced them to go in a different direction. As long as I was there, I'd fill most of the seats and sell a lot of jerseys, even during terrible seasons. From a business standpoint there was no reason to make a change. But with me gone, they were forced to regroup."[124]

This effort to "regroup" is where Matt Millen enters the picture. During the mid-1990s, Bill Ford Jr joined the team's management as vice chairman. He was instrumental in bringing about the Detroit stadiums deal that resulted in Ford Field for the Lions and Comerica Park for the Tigers. He was also involved in relocating the Lions' offices and training facilities from Pontiac to Allen Park. In addition, Bill Jr represented the Lions at the NFL owners' meetings, and that's where he first heard of Matt Millen. During discussions on various issues, people asked, "What does Millen think?" "What does Millen say about it?"[125] Bill Jr wondered: who is Millen? He asked around and was told "Millen was a student of the game, knowledgeable of the championship nuances that always eluded the Lions."[126]

Matt Millen had been an All-American defensive tackle at Pennsylvania State University before being drafted by the Oakland Raiders in 1980. Converted to linebacker, he went on to have a twelve-year career in the NFL and earned four Super Bowl rings while playing for the

Raiders (2), San Francisco 49ers (1), and Washington Redskins (1). His final season was 1991 when he was a member of the Washington team that beat the Lions in the NFC title game.[127] When his playing days were over, Millen moved into broadcasting and served as an analyst covering NFL games for CBS, Fox, and Westwood One Radio. Millen was a popular commentator who impressed audiences with his knowledge of the game, sense of humor, and interesting stories. By the late 1990s, he was Fox Sports' #2 football analyst and heir-apparent to the legendary John Madden.

At some point during 1999, Bill Ford Jr pitched to his father the idea of hiring Millen to run the Lions. Bill Sr was interested and made an offer to Millen. Millen's initial response was, "Mr. Ford, I really appreciate this, but I'm not qualified. I've had no training. I know that game of football—but there's a lot more to it than that."[128]

Bill Sr's reply: "You're smart. You'll figure it out."

Millen wasn't hired that year because the offer was pulled when Head Coach Bobby Ross told Bill Sr he'd resign if Millen was hired. The plan was moved to the back burner. The 1999 Lions slipped into the playoffs with an 8-8 record but lost to Washington in the first round.

Ross resigned during the 2000 season, citing health issues as the reason. He also said he'd been unable to change the team's culture. Assistant Gary Moeller was elevated to head coach and given a contract to finish out the season and continue two more years. Moeller's team won four of their next seven games to give the Lions a 9-6 record with one game remaining. To qualify for the playoffs they had to defeat the 4-11 Chicago Bears in the season finale. However, the Lions lost 20-23 on a last-second Bears' field goal.

After the game, Bill Sr asked Bill Jr if he still had Millen's phone number. Later, Bill Sr told reporters: "[We've] been stuck on dead-center for quite a few years…So let's roll the dice and take a gamble."[129] Bill Jr added: "We haven't been bad, we haven't been great, we're about in the middle, 0-5 in playoff games and that's just not good enough."[130]

A Bold Experiment

Putting someone with no NFL coaching or front office experience in charge of the Lions was a bold, outrageous idea that appealed to many in Detroit's media and fan base. After all, what the Lions had been doing hadn't worked, so why not try something new? Millen accepted the Lions' offer and was named president and chief executive officer in January 2001. He was also the de-facto general manager. His five-year contract at $3 million per year made him the highest paid executive in the NFL. The immediate loser was General Manager Chuck Schmidt who retired.

Lions' fans were excited. The pot had been stirred. A well-respected, popular, knowledgeable football man was in charge of the Lions. Surely better days were ahead!

What Went Wrong?

The team's performance during the Matt Millen Era was truly abysmal. The data show what happened: six consecutive seasons with double-digit losses, a season high of seven wins (in 2007), and defensive and offensive rankings consistently at or near the bottom of the league. The team's overall record was 31-84, and the losses included an (at that time) NFL record twenty-four game road losing streak from 2001-2003. In 2006, an unnamed NFL executive told the *Boston Globe* that Millen's "got the worst record in history from a general manger and he'll have that record forever."[131]

No one ever doubted Matt Millen's knowledge of football. The problem was applying that knowledge to the management position, and then turning the Lions into a winner. Sportswriter Jerry Green—an admirer of Millen—said Millen was "out of his element."[132] Looking back years later, Millen himself acknowledged being "in over my head."[133]

Millen made mistakes in several areas. First and foremost was player acquisition. He made some bad free agent moves, but perhaps worse were his draft choices. The first year (2001) went well as the first three picks—Jeff Backus, Dominic Raiola, and Shaun Rogers—became long-term starters and Rogers went on to become an All-Pro. The next several drafts went badly, and a look at Millen's first-round selections gives an idea of what happened. The Lions' first pick in 2002 was University of Oregon quarterback Joey Harrington who Millen hoped would become the franchise quarterback. Harrington felt intense pressure the moment he arrived in Detroit: "Literally when I walked off the jetway…the day after the draft, this stranger welcomed me and then said: 'The two toughest jobs in Detroit are playing quarterback for the Lions and goalie for the Red Wings.' Then he slapped me on the back…and said, 'We haven't had a quarterback since Bobby Layne, good luck.'"[134]

Harrington was named starting quarterback three games into his rookie season. Thrown into the frying pan early, he had a weak supporting cast and his skill set didn't match up well with the spread-type offense the Lions were using at the time. The team fared poorly, Harrington had problems completing passes, and his self-confidence slipped away. "By the time I left [Detroit in 2005], I was a shell of the player I once was," said Harrington. "In the NFL (and especially at the quarterback position), if you don't have confidence, you're done."[135]

Millen had been a self-motivated player who didn't need coaches riding herd over him because he did that to himself. The problem was he tended to think everyone else was like him, so his draft selections emphasized athletic ability and underplayed attitude and commitment. As a result, some of the Lions' high draft choices were talented athletes with motivation issues. Exhibit A was Charles Rogers, the Lions' first pick in 2003, and Exhibit B was Mike Williams, the first-round pick in 2005. Rogers was a star wide receiver at Michigan State who Millen chose over Andre Johnson (who went on to major success with the Houston Texans) because of Rogers' local connection. Rogers was from Saginaw and Millen thought it "would be good for the franchise—a hometown kid."[136] Rogers' contract included a $14.4 million signing bonus. "Charles wasn't a strong person," said Millen. "I miscalculated all the people that would latch onto him, especially being so close to his hometown."[137]

Rogers had a host of problems, some bad luck, some brought on by himself. He started out well, catching 22 passes and scoring 3 touchdowns in his first five games. Then it unraveled: he broke his collarbone in practice and was out for the rest of the season. Millen allowed Rogers to leave the team and go home to Saginaw (a decision Millen later regretted). Rogers was back in 2004 and in Chicago on opening day re-broke his collarbone on the third play of the game. He then became addicted to Vicodin and in 2005 failed three drug tests before being served a four-game suspension for violating the NFL's substance abuse policy. He never played again that season, and the Lions released him the following year.

The team did better with Roy Williams, their first-round pick in 2004.[138] Another wide receiver (we'll get to that later), Williams was from the University of Texas and caught fifty-four passes during his rookie year with the Lions. He went on to have a solid NFL career and was named a Pro-Bowl alternate in 2007. Millen, however, was never a huge fan: "Roy didn't like to work. I had him in my office all the time."[139] William was traded away in 2008 after Millen was fired. The Dallas Cowboys had long coveted Williams and offered the Lions a deal too good to turn down.[140]

In the first-round of the 2005 draft, the Lions chose another wide receiver named Williams. Mike Williams (no relation to Roy) from the University of Southern California is notable because Millen didn't plan to select him. The Lions badly needed a pass rusher and Millen intended to draft DeMarcus Ware.

On draft day, Millen and the Lions' coaches and scouts were in agreement about choosing Ware. But when the moment arrived, Mike Williams was still available. The coaches and scouts changed their minds: they wanted Williams.

"I listened to the group," said Millen. "They thought if they got Mike Williams and paired him with Roy Williams…we could do all these things…[W]hen we were just about ready to pick, I had DeMarcus Ware on the phone." Millen buckled to the pressure: "I said, 'all right, take Mike Williams.' My son was in the draft room…and that's when he punched me [in the stomach]. What a dope I was."[141]

When Mike Williams arrived in Detroit, the Lions told him he was overweight and gave him a target weight he could never achieve. He caught a touchdown pass on opening day but it was his only TD of the season. During his two years with the Lions he caught 37 passes and scored 2 touchdowns. Millen was soon fed-up with him. "His rookie year, I think I fined him every cent of his salary…It was ridiculous. He didn't care."[142] In 2007, Williams asked to be traded and the Lions sent him to Oakland.

Millen's final first-round picks went better. Linebacker Ernie Sims was the selection in 2006, and he started on the team for four years. Then, in 2007, Calvin Johnson (HOF) was drafted out of Georgia Tech. There was widespread agreement that Johnson was the best athlete available, but fans were upset because he was yet another wide receiver. Some felt the Lions should've traded down to accumulate more picks because they needed help everywhere. Johnson, of course, worked out extremely well: he holds the Lions' records for total receptions (731) and receiving yards (11,619). During his nine-year career with the Lions he averaged 15.9 yards per catch and scored 83 touchdowns. In 2021, he became the second-youngest former player to be inducted into the Professional Football Hall of Fame.

Millen's final draft was in 2008. The Lions' first pick was Gosder Cherilus, an offensive tackle who started for the team for four years.[143]

The drafting problems weren't confined to first-rounders. During Millen's time in Detroit, he oversaw eight drafts and selected sixty-two players. When he was fired in late September 2008, twenty-seven of his draftees were on the Lions, five were on other NFL teams, and thirty were out of the NFL. At the time of Millen's firing only two draftees, Shaun Rogers and Roy Williams, had made the Pro Bowl.[144] Detroit sportswriter Nicholas Cotsonika sums up player acquisition during the Matt Millen Era this way: "[U]nder Millen, the Lions had too many talented players with not enough character, and too many character players with not enough talent."[145]

Team Building

Another problem was Millen's team-building skills. He's been widely excoriated on this point and the oft-cited evidence is his use of four first-round draft picks on wide receivers over a six-year span. Conventional wisdom in the NFL is that teams are built on both sides of the ball: you start with a quarterback, an offensive line to protect him, and defenders. Wide receivers and running backs are important, but they are also plentiful.

One way to gauge the importance of the various position players on an NFL team is to look at how much they're paid. Here are data on 2021 average salaries across the NFL by position, ranked from high to low:[146]

Quarterback	$5.7 million
Offensive Tackle	$3.3 million
Defensive End	$2.9 million
Defensive Tackle	$2.7 million
Offensive Guard	$2.5 million
Wide Receiver	$2.5 million
Linebacker	$2.4 million
Center	$2.3 million
Safety	$2.2 million
Cornerback	$2.2 million
Tight End	$2.0 million
Running Back	$1.7 million
Place Kicker	$1.9 million
Punter	$1.5 million
Long Snapper	$0.9 million

While many factors go into determining these numbers—value to the teams, abundance vs scarcity, players' experience—they provide an idea of where to focus when building a team. Wide receivers are valuable, but not as valuable as quarterbacks and linemen. Receivers may handle the ball around six times per game; on a huge day the number might be twelve.[147] Quarterbacks handle the ball on every offensive play. Linemen are central to the outcome of every play. The salaries suggest that team building involves allocating prime resources toward quarterbacks and linemen unless exceptional players are available at other positions. Drafting three consecutive wide receivers in the first round is not a sound strategy.

During his time in Detroit, Millen seemingly knew this, forgot it, and relearned it. He started out using first round picks on an offensive lineman and a quarterback, then became enamored with wide receivers. At the end he chose an offensive lineman.

The Parade of Coaches

Gary Moeller had two years left on his head coaching contract when Millen arrived. Millen promptly fired Moeller and replaced him with San Francisco's offensive coordinator Marty Mornhinweg. Mornhinweg was big on designing plays but, like Millen, tended to think everyone was self-motivated. He took over a team short on talent and in need of motivation which was not his forte.

During Mornhinweg's two years as head coach the team went 5-27. The 2001 Lions lost their first twelve games and ended the season 2-14. They scored 270 points and gave up 424. The 2002 team—playing the inaugural season at Ford Field—was 3-5 at the midway point of the season, then lost their last eight to finish 3-13. One of those losses was the infamous road game against the Bears when the Lions won the overtime coin flip, then told the referee they wanted to defend the windward end zone. The Bears received the kick, drove down the field, and kicked a game-winning field goal into the wind. This game, which is seared into the memories of many Lions' fans, is discussed in Chapter 10. At the end of the season Millen said Mornhinweg would return for the 2003 season, but then fired him twenty-seven days later. Many suspect Mornhinweg was let go because a better coach had become available.

The San Francisco 49ers had just fired Steve Mariucci. The head coach there since 1997, Mariucci led the 49ers to several playoff appearances but no Super Bowls. Millen hired him on February 4, 2003, and gave him big money: a five-year contract worth $25 million.

Mariucci fared slightly better than Mornhinweg, but not well enough to last. Determined to install the West Coast pass-control offense, he didn't have the players to make it work. In his first season the team went 5-11. In 2004 they finished 6-10.

Before the 2005 season began, Bill Ford Sr—with Bill Jr's support—extended Millen's contract another five years. Lions' fans were aghast: the team's record under Millen was 16-48 *and his contract was extended?* Losers again that season, the Lions were 4-6 heading into Thanksgiving Day. They suffered a humiliating 7-27 loss to the Atlanta Falcons on national television and Millen had seen enough. He fired Mariucci and elevated defensive coordinator Dick Jauron to interim head coach. The Lions finished the season 5-11.

By this point, the Lions' scene had become a dark comedy. Matt Millen had hired and fired a long list of front office staff, head coaches, assistant coaches, and players. He'd fired almost everyone he could fire except himself. And the Bill Fords were still overseeing the operation. There was no consistent plan within the organization; by the end of Millen's seven-plus years the coaching parade had included five offensive coordinators and five defensive coordinators, each with his own system. It's hard to imagine a football team being more badly managed.

The Fans Revolt

On December 4, 2005, the Lions met the Vikings at Ford Field. It was Dick Jauron's first game as interim head coach and memorable because it served as the backdrop for the 2005 Ford Field Fan Revolt. They say revolutions need a spark; this one was ignited by a fan named Aaron Tobin who brought to the game two signs he'd made with his PC and printer. Tobin said the signs were "maybe three feet long." Both said, "Fire Millen!"[148]

Upon arrival at Ford Field, Tobin handed one of the signs to a friend and kept the other. They held up the signs, and the friend had his confiscated by stadium security during the first half. Meanwhile, the game started well for the Lions. They kicked a field goal on the opening possession. However, their lead was short-lived because after the kickoff the Vikings started on their own 20-yard line. On their first play from scrimmage quarterback Brad Johnson threw a pass down the right sideline to Koren Robinson for an 80-yard touchdown reception.

The Lions were down 6-14 at the start of the second-half. As the game went on the fans, dismayed by the Lions' performance, began chanting, "Fire Millen." Meanwhile, Tobin, who was still holding his sign, was approached by stadium security. He was told to hand it over or be ejected. In a defiant act, Tobin gave the sign to another fan. Security went after that fan, who handed it off to another fan. Thus, a chase began that was ultimately won by security when they managed to grab the sign. The crowd cheered and booed throughout, and then used markers to write "Fire Millen" on all sorts of objects including pizza boxes and paper bags. Security confiscated more signs. Another chase broke out, this time a fan was running through the aisles holding up his "Fire Millen" sign with security in pursuit. The crowd and several players watched, and television cameras covered the action. The man was eventually tackled by security and escorted from the building. The Lions lost 16-21.

Television, newspapers, sports talk radio, and the internet were soon abuzz. The mantra was, "fire Millen" and most everyone piled on. There was one home game left and the angry fan contingent wanted to make it count. A local radio station planned an angry fan parade—a "Millen Man March"—prior to the December 18th contest against the Cincinnati Bengals. Fans were urged to bring signs and wear Bengals' orange instead of Lions' blue.

Several hundred fans took part in the pregame parade. One fan carried a piece of lumber with a dummy of Matt Millen hanging in effigy from the end. Many others had signs, and they chanted phrases including, "Fire Millen" during their march to Ford Field. Once the game began, however, the crowd was mostly quiet because the contest soon became a blowout. Just before the opening kickoff, Lions' return man R.W. McQuarters urged on the crowd by waving his arms. He then fumbled the kick, the Bengals recovered, and moments later were leading 3-0. The Lions lost 17-41.

Another Coach Needed

The Lions ended the 2005 season with a 5-11 record. In January 2006, Millen interviewed candidates for the head coaching position, Dick Jauron among them. Jauron didn't receive an offer but landed on his feet. He became the head coach of the Buffalo Bills which is notable because it made Jauron the first Lions' head coach since Buddy Parker to get another head coaching job in the NFL.

Millen hired Rod Marinelli who'd been assistant head coach and defensive line coach at Tampa Bay. During Marinelli's first season the Lions went 3-13. There was improvement in 2007 when the offense perked up. John Kitna played quarterback and the team started well; when the Lions beat the Denver Broncos on November 4th their record improved to 6-2. They were on-track to reach the playoffs.

However, the Lions went cold after that. The defense fell apart, the offense stagnated, and the Lions proceeded to lose seven of their last eight games and finish the season 7-9. It was an epic collapse highlighted by a pass defense that allowed opposing quarterbacks to complete 70 percent of their pass attempts.

The 2008 season is the subject of the next chapter so we'll hold off on details. When the Lions lost their first three, Bill Ford Jr realized it was time to make a change. The team had given up 113 points in three games and it was clear another losing season was on the way. Hiring Millen had been his idea, so it seems fitting that he was involved in getting Millen fired. After the Lions lost to San Francisco by a score of 13-31, Bill Ford Jr told a reporter while a television camera was running: "[The game] was an embarrassment. The fans deserve better. If I had the authority, I would have fired the general manager."

Was Bill Jr forcing his father's hand? Or had Bill Sr already made the decision to fire Millen? The Fords never said. Whatever the case, the Fords decided it was time to part ways with Millen. Bill Sr fired Matt Millen on September 24, 2008, and elevated Martin Mayhew to interim general manager. The Lions' bold management experiment was over. Lions' fans expressed widespread joy. Little did they know the misery would continue unabated through the remainder of the season.

The Matt Millen Era was an utter disaster, and it dragged on for years. It was one thing to employ a man who drove the franchise into the ground, and something else to keep him around for over seven seasons. It required a peculiar combination of an owner who liked his failing team executive and didn't want to fire him, and a failing team executive who was so stubborn he would never admit failure and quit.

In 2018, Matt Millen reflected on what happened: "Really, when I take steps back, I was not ready at all. Not even close. I was in over my head. And by the time I figured it out, it wasn't necessarily too late, but we were in pretty deep."[149]

THE MATT MILLEN ERA, 2001-2008[*]

YEAR	LIONS' RECORD	OFFENSE RANK	DEFENSE RANK
2001	2-14	16th	26th
2002	3-13	28th	31st
2003	5-11	32nd	24th
2004	6-10	24th	22nd
2005	5-11	27th	20th
2006	3-13	22nd	28th
2007	7-9	19th	32nd
2008	0-3	22nd	31st

*Offensive and Defensive rankings are among all NFL teams. There were 31 teams in 2001, 32 teams beginning 2002. Millen was fired after the third game of the 2008 season and rankings shown for that season are after three games. The team ended 2008 at 0-16 and ranked 27th in team offense and 32nd in team defense.

LIONS' FIRST ROUND DRAFT PICKS, 2001-2008

YEAR	PLAYER	POSITION	COLLEGE
2001	Jeff Backus	OT	Michigan
2002	Joey Harrington	QB	Oregon
2003	Charles Rogers	WR	Michigan State
2004	Roy Williams	WR	Texas
	Kevin Jones	RB	Virginia Tech
2005	Mike Williams	WR	U of Southern Cal
2006	Ernie Sims	LB	Florida State
2007	Calvin Johnson	WR	Georgia Tech
2008	Gosder Cherilus	OT	Boston College

Chapter 8
2008: A Season for the Ages

There's bad, and there's *bad*. The 2008 Detroit Lions were *bad*.

The Lions' 2008 season is best viewed as the horrible final act of the Matt Millen Era. Millen was fired after the third loss of the season, but the players, coaching staff, and front-office personnel he'd assembled were still around to continue their losing ways. And lose they did, thirteen more times to end a "perfect season" with an 0-16 record. The losses were caused by the same things Lions' fans have seen for years: missed tackles, missed blocks, dropped passes, bad kicks, fumbles, interceptions, penalties, bad luck, often at critical moments in a game. The difference is that in 2008 these things went on all season, from opening day in Atlanta to the season finale in Green Bay.

Winless seasons are rare in modern times, but they were common in the NFL's early days. From the league's founding in 1920 through 1929, twenty-four teams had winless seasons. However, it was a different era; teams played fewer games per season which raised the probability of not posting a win. Also, many NFL teams played a mixed schedule against both NFL and semi-pro teams. Since only games against NFL opponents counted in their NFL records, some teams were winless because they played and lost to a small number of NFL teams in a season, giving them a league record of 0-1 or 0-2. Another reason why winless seasons were common was because many NFL teams were financially strapped. An open market for players existed (i.e., there were no limits on salaries) so teams earning profits could pay more for talent than teams which were losing money. This made the strong teams stronger and weak teams weaker.

The situation changed in the 1930s. The Great Depression killed off many of the financially weakest teams which made winless seasons less likely. In fact, there was only one winless team during the decade—the 1934 Cincinnati Reds were 0-8. Then, in 1936, the NFL went to the draft system for college players. The brainchild of Philadelphia Eagles' owner Bert Bell, the college draft was designed to accomplish two goals: create a cartel among NFL teams to prevent them from bidding against each other for players coming out of college, and promote parity among teams. The NFL owners created a system (very similar to the one used today) where once a college player is drafted by an NFL team, no other NFL teams will bid for his services. The NFL owners never consulted the players about the system, they simply imposed it. The parity feature comes from the draft order: in each round of the draft, the team with the worst record during the previous season chooses first, the second-worst team chooses second, and so on until the best team chooses last. The idea behind parity was to attract fans: NFL owners understood that more competitive games would increase fan interest. Ironically, the NFL's worst team in 1935—Bert Bell's Eagles—picked first in all nine rounds of the 1936 draft yet were unable to sign any of those players. Back in those days salaries offered to players were so low (a typical NFL salary was $250 per game) that in many cases draftees could earn as much or more in the business world and not risk injury while doing it.[150]

World War II brought back winless seasons. During the War (1941-45), team rosters were ravaged by the military's need for young men. The quality of play in the NFL plummeted, winless seasons returned, and there was talk of cancelling the NFL for the duration of the conflict. But football continued in a diminished state, including in Detroit where the 1942 Lions posted the NFL's first winless season since 1934.

Here's the current (through 2022) list of NFL winless seasons post 1934:

1942	Detroit Lions	0-11
1943	Chicago Cardinals	0-10
1944	Card/Pitt[151]	0-10
1944	Brooklyn Tigers	0-10
1960	Dallas Cowboys	0-11-1
1976	Tampa Bay Buccaneers	0-14
1982	Baltimore Colts	0-8-1
2008	Detroit Lions	0-16
2017	Cleveland Browns	0-16

[151]

The disruptions caused by World War II explain the first four entries. The 1960 Dallas Cowboys were a first-year expansion team, as were the 1976 Tampa Bay Buccaneers. The 1982 Baltimore Colts were winless during a strike-shortened season. This means that just two teams listed, the 2008 Lions and 2017 Browns, meet the Gold Standard of Winless Seasons: modern-era established teams, playing a full season in peacetime, and losing every game while doing it.[152]

What are the Odds?

Since World War II ended, NFL teams have played approximately 1,800 team-seasons. During that time five teams have gone winless which is 0.27 percent of the total, or one out of 370. In other words, based on past history, in today's world of thirty-two NFL teams, one of them goes winless an average of every 11-12 years. If we narrow it down to non-expansion teams during non-strike shortened seasons, the average is once every twenty-eight years. No matter how it's measured we're talking low-probability event. Accomplishing the feat requires a rare combination of low talent and consistently bad luck.

How did the 2008 Lions do it? Here's a short answer: by having one of the worst defenses in NFL history.

The defensive unit posted eye-popping numbers. Over the season, opponents scored 517 points which works out to an average of 32.3 points per game. The Lions gave up 69 touchdowns. Opposing offenses completed 303 passes out of 443 attempts which is a completion rate of 68.4 percent. Those aerial attacks scored 25 touchdowns while Lions' defenders intercepted *4 passes*. Opponents' offenses gained an average of 6.4 yards per play. Their running backs averaged 5.1 yards (by point of comparison, Barry Sanders' career average was 5.0 yards).

The Lions' offense was bad too. While opponents were scoring their 69 touchdowns the Lions scored 29. Detroit scored 268 points, for an average of 16.75 per game. They completed 55 percent of their passes. Their quarterbacks were sacked 52 times. It took the Lions until the seventh game of the season to score a point during the first quarter of a game. Their anemic offense combined with the historically bad defense provided Lions' fans with a lost season.

Oddly enough, Detroit was 4-0 during the preseason. Of course, preseason games mean little, but it gave the Lions the illusion of momentum heading into the regular season. Most football prognosticators didn't expect much from the 2008 team given how the 2007 season had ended. Over the last eight games in 2007, the Lions were 1-7 and the collapse was due in large part to having the league's worst-ranked defense. There was little reason to think the 2008 version would be better. On offense, there was another new coordinator, Jon Kitna was returning at quarterback, the running backs were veteran Rudi Johnson and rookie Kevin Smith, and the wide receiver corps included Roy Williams and second-year player Calvin Johnson. The offensive line had given up 117 sacks the previous two seasons, and four of the five starters from 2007 were back in 2008. Forecasters did not expect a successful campaign in 2008, but none predicted 0-16.

There was, however, one clairvoyant: starting quarterback Jon Kitna. According to Calvin Johnson, before the 2008 season began, "[Jon Kitna] left the meeting room one day, and he told the coaches and the whole team that we're not gonna win a game if we go into the season with [this] system. Somebody should have listened. Because we were 0-16 after that."[153]

Slow Out of the Box

Presumably, the system Kitna was referring to was the Lions' offensive plan heading into the season. The Lions intended to focus on running the ball so opponents would play one deep safety instead of two. This would allow the Lions to complete occasional long passes to their deep-threat wide receivers. At least that was the plan.

The reality was that the Lions' offensive line couldn't open the holes needed to mount an effective running game. In fact, the running game was so ineffective that opponents were able to defend it and still have two deep safeties. Thus, the Lions ended up with the worst of both worlds: a running game that couldn't gain yards with consistency, and opponents playing two deep safeties to defend the deep pass threat.[154]

The season started badly, and defensive problems were obvious from the get-go. As noted earlier, the Lions gave up 113 points while losing their first three games. Then Matt Millen was fired. The fourth game was a 7-34 blowout loss to the Bears. During that game, Jon Kitna's back flared up and he was done for the season.

Dan Orlovsky stepped in and started at quarterback against the Vikings on October 12th. The contest in Minneapolis is notable because it was the game the Lions came closest to winning. Late in the first quarter the Vikings fumbled deep in the Lions' end and Detroit recovered on the 1-yard line. After two incomplete passes, Orlovsky dropped back into the end zone to attempt another throw. Vikings' pass rusher Jared Allen broke through the line and pursued Orlovsky who ran out the back of the end zone for a 2-point safety.

Orlovsky didn't realize what had happened. "When they started blowing the whistle, I was like 'Did we false start or were they offsides or something?' And I looked, and I was just like 'You're an idiot'…Just a dumb play by me."[155]

The event was captured on camera and is now one of the most famous moments in recent Lions' history. The play also gave the Vikings a 2-point lead that turned out to be the margin of victory. But on this day the Lions didn't wilt under pressure. The defense held the Vikings scoreless during the second quarter and the Lions' offensive produced a field goal. The Lions led at halftime 3-2.

The teams traded touchdowns in the third quarter. The play of the game occurred with 2:15 left in the fourth quarter and the Lions leading 10-9. On a second and 20 from the Minnesota 32-yard line, Vikings' quarterback Gus Frerotte threw the ball down the right sideline toward receiver Aundrae Allison. Lions' defensive back Leigh Bodden was on the coverage. The pass was incomplete, but an official threw a penalty flag for defensive pass interference.

Boden said he looked for the ball and never touched the receiver. "I did everything right," he said. The Lions were outraged by the call which gave the Vikings a 42-yard gain and set them up for the game-winning field goal. "Those types of games, you have to win," said Head Coach Rod Marinelli. "You fight, but you fight to win."[156] The Lions lost 10-12.

The next few games were close but the Lions kept losing.[157] Orlovsky was still the starter on November 2nd in Chicago when the Lions scored 23 points in the second quarter and led at halftime 23-13. But the Bears mounted a second-half comeback by scoring 2 touchdowns and holding the Lions scoreless. Drew Stanton made his NFL debut at quarterback the following week against Jacksonville. Stanton was a 2007 second-round draft pick from Michigan State. His first pass completion came in the first quarter and was a 1-yard touchdown pass to John Owens. It gave the Lions a 7-3 lead, but in the second quarter the Jaguars scored 21 unanswered points. Detroit lost 14-38 and fell to 0-9.

By October it was clear the season was heading down the toilet, and the Lions were looking for another quarterback. They focused on retired veteran Dante Culpepper who'd last played for Minnesota. Culpepper signed a contract on November 3rd and started against the Carolina Panthers on November 16th. He had a respectable performance, but the Lions' defense had another bad day. The team led 7-0 at the end of the first quarter, but in the second quarter the Panthers scored 3 touchdowns while the Lions managed 3 field goals and went on to lose 22-31. Culpepper started again a week later against Tampa Bay. The Lions jumped out to a 17-0 first-quarter lead—their largest positive margin of the season. It disappeared when the Buccaneers scored 35 unanswered points and went on to win 38-20.

On November 27th the Tennessee Titans administered the Lions a Thanksgiving Day defeat of 47-10. The 47 points scored by Tennessee are the most the Lions have ever given up on the holiday, and the 37-point margin of defeat set a record for being the most lopsided Lions' loss ever on Thanksgiving Day. The Lions fell to 0-12.

Culpepper was injured in the rematch against Minnesota which the Lions lost 16-20. Dan Orlovsky started the last three games of the season: losses to Indianapolis and New Orleans, and the finale at Green Bay. The Lions entered the Packers' game 0-15 and desperately wanting to avoid making history. They were on the brink of doing something that no other NFL team had ever done before.

In terms of the standings, the game was meaningless for both teams. The Packers were 5-10 and out of the playoffs but didn't want to be the only team to lose to the Lions. Packers' fans— who'd displayed "Keep Millen!" signs in prior seasons—turned out to see their team try to hold the Lions winless. Over 70,000 attended in 22-degree weather and chanted "0 and 16" while the Packers jumped out to a 14-0 first-quarter lead before prevailing 31-21. The Lions left the field to chants of "Purrfect Season!"

The nightmare season was finally over.

Postscript

No one was surprised, least of all Head Coach Rod Marinelli, when he was fired the next day. Most of his assistants were also fired, and many of the players were released.[158] Yet management survived. Interim General Manager Martin Mayhew was retained as general manager, and Tom Lewand, who'd been executive vice president, was elevated to president. Bill Ford Sr remained in control, and son Bill Jr continued as vice chairman.

While the 2008 season was a disaster for the Detroit Lions, two good things came out of it. The first is that Calvin Johnson established himself as a star. Playing on a very bad team, he caught 78 passes for 1,331 yards (an average of 17.1 per reception) and scored 12 touchdowns. Johnson clearly had a bright future in the NFL. The second positive item was that the NFL's worst team in 2008 would get the first pick in the 2009 draft.

The Lions needed a franchise quarterback to build the team around. Among draft-eligible players, the University of Georgia's Matthew Stafford was considered the best at the position. To make it even better, he'd graduated from the same high school as Bobby Layne and Doak Walker. It was an obvious decision that even the Lions couldn't mess up, and on April 25, 2009, they chose Stafford first in the NFL draft.

DETROIT LIONS 2008 SEASON

PRESEASON

August 7	Detroit Lions 13, New York Giants 10	Ford Field
August 17	Detroit Lions 27, Cincinnati Bengals 10	Paul Brown Stadium
August 23	Detroit Lions 26, Cleveland Browns 6	Ford Field
August 28	Detroit Lions 14, Buffalo Bills 6	R. Wilson Stadium

Preseason Record: 4-0 **Detroit Points Scored: 80** **Detroit Points Allowed: 32**

REGULAR SEASON

September 7	Atlanta Falcons 34, Detroit Lions 21	Georgia Dome
September 14	Green Bay Packers 48, Detroit Lions 25	Ford Field
September 21	San Francisco 49ers 31, Detroit Lions 13	Candlestick Park
October 5	Chicago Bears 34, Detroit Lions 7	Ford Field
October 12	Minnesota Vikings 12, Detroit Lions 10	HHH Metrodome
October 19	Houston Texans 28, Detroit Lions 21	Reliant Stadium
October 26	Washington Redskins 25, Detroit Lions 17	Ford Field
November 2	Chicago Bears 27, Detroit Lions 23	Soldier Field
November 9	Jacksonville Jaguars 38, Detroit Lions 14	Ford Field
November 16	Carolina Panthers 31, Detroit Lions 22	B of A Stadium
November 23	Tampa Bay Buccaneers 38, Detroit Lions 20	Ford Field
November 27	Tennessee Titans 47, Detroit Lions 10	Ford Field
December 7	Minnesota Vikings 20, Detroit Lions 16	Ford Field
December 14	Indianapolis Colts 31, Detroit Lions 21	Lucas Oil Stadium
December 21	New Orleans Saints 42, Detroit Lions 7	Ford Field
December 28	Green Bay Packers 31, Detroit Lions 21	Lambeau Field

Regular Season Record: 0-16 **Detroit Points Scored: 268** **Detroit Points Allowed: 517**

Chapter 9
Four Head Coaches in Fourteen Years

Since 2008 the Lions have mostly wallowed in mediocrity and worse. Over the thirteen seasons from 2009-22 the team's record was 91-133-1, or a win-rate of 40 percent. There were two seasons of double-digit wins and three playoff appearances. As expected, the 2011 and 2016 Lions didn't get beyond the postseason's first round. However, many fans thought the 2014 team had the talent to advance. But it didn't happen because in the wild card game against Dallas the Lions were torpedoed by bad play at critical moments and that awful Lions' luck.

Meanwhile, the coaching parade continued. The organization had four head coaches (six if you include an interim head coach and an acting-interim head coach). The revolving door kept spinning and through it passed coaches, general managers, and players who were part of rebuilding programs that couldn't achieve sustained success. It's been the same old Detroit Lions' story, although this time it might have a different ending because a new generation of Ford family ownership took control in 2020. The early returns from the 2021 and 2022 seasons are promising so it's possible the future will differ from the past.

Here's a synopsis of the Lions' fortunes since 2008.

Jim Schwartz

The housecleaning that took place following the 2008 season resulted in a new head coach, new offensive and defensive coordinators, and several new assistants. There was major turnover on the roster as well; fewer than half the 2008 Lions were on the team in 2009.

Since Detroit was ranked dead last in NFL team defense during the 2007 and 2008 seasons, it's not surprising the new head coach was a defensive specialist. Jim Schwartz had been an NFL assistant since 1996 and spent his last eight years as defensive coordinator for the Tennessee Titans. The Lions signed him to a four-year contract worth $11 million.

Schwartz walked into an unusual situation. If ever a team was ready for a new beginning it was the 2009 Detroit Lions. There was nowhere to go but up, and no one would've batted an eye if Schwartz had released nearly the entire roster of players. Furthermore, the Lions had the number one pick in the upcoming draft. Schwartz was presented with a rare opportunity to remake a team almost from scratch and do it for a fan base that didn't expect an instant winner. If he could create success in Detroit he'd be celebrated throughout the NFL.

The 2009 draft was a good start. The Lions chose several players who became long-term starters. As expected, the number-one pick was quarterback Matthew Stafford. The Lions also had the first-round pick they'd acquired from Dallas in the Roy Williams' trade and used on tight end Brandon Pettigrew. In addition, they selected defensive back Louis Delmas, linebacker DeAndre Levy, and defensive lineman Sammie Hill.

Stafford was named starting quarterback before the season began. He went through a steep learning curve while playing behind a weak offensive line. Fortunately, there were talented receivers—led by Calvin Johnson—to catch his passes. The Lions won two games in 2009: a victory at Ford Field on September 27th over the Washington Redskins which broke Detroit's 19-game losing streak, and a stirring 38-37 victory against Cleveland on November 22nd when

Stafford returned to the field after being injured and on the final play threw his fifth touchdown pass of the day for the win. The Lions ended the season 2-14 and had the second pick in the upcoming draft.

They selected University of Nebraska defensive tackle Ndamukong Suh in the first-round of the 2010 draft. Suh was an immediate impact player with 10 sacks and 66 tackles and named NFL Defensive Rookie of the Year and First-Team All Pro. However, his sterling play wasn't enough to prevent the Lions from starting badly: they dropped their first four, then muddled along to a 2-10 record by early December. Then they perked up and closed out the season with a four-game winning streak to finish 6-10. The rebuilding program showed signs of success.

More improvement was expected in 2011. Conventional wisdom in the NFL says that talent shows itself by the third year, and the Lions' first round picks from 2009 were entering their third year as was Head Coach Jim Schwartz. The early returns were outstanding: Detroit started 5-0 (their best early-season showing since the 1950s) before cooling off. They did something else remarkable: they won five road games. Those road wins were matched by an equal number at home so they finished the season 10-6. It was the Lions' best record since 1995 and put them in the playoffs as a wild card.

The Lions relied heavily on the passing game. The offensive line had trouble opening holes and several running backs were injured, so roughly two-thirds of the offensive plays were pass attempts. The aerial game accounted for 76 percent of yards gained. Stafford threw for over 5,000 yards and Calvin Johnson was the target for 1,681 of them. Dependence on the aerial attack and the league's 23rd worst defense are the reasons why the Lions weren't expected to go far in the playoffs.

They faced the Saints in New Orleans in the first round. It was a rematch of their game on December 4th that the Saints won 31-17 by building a 24-7 halftime lead and cruising the rest of the way. The playoff game followed a somewhat different script: the Lions played well in the first half and went to the locker room ahead 14-10. The lead would've been larger if a referee call hadn't gone against them. Detroit was leading 14-7 with 5:37 left in the second quarter when defensive lineman Willie Young hit Saints' quarterback Drew Brees and forced a fumble. The Lions' Justin Durant picked up the ball and had an open path to the end zone, but an official blew the play dead and called an incomplete pass. That official was overruled and the play called a fumble, but the opportunity was lost. The Lions earned no points from it.

New Orleans made the necessary halftime adjustments and came out blazing in the third quarter. Detroit's defense was overmatched and when the game was over the Saints had scored on seven of their ten possessions and racked up 626 yards of total offense. The final score was Saints 45, Lions 28.

That season was the high point of the Jim Schwartz era. In 2012, the defense slipped to 27th in the league and the offense moved backwards as well. Detroit was 4-4 after beating Jacksonville on November 4th, but it was the last victory of the season. The Lions lost their final eight games and finished 4-12. One item of note is that kicker Jason Hanson retired after twenty-one years with the team.

The Lions did well in the 2013 draft by selecting defensive lineman Ezekiel Ansah, defensive back Darius Slay, and offensive lineman Larry Warford. The season started well: after nine games the Lions were 6-3. However, the season turned sour on November 17th in Pittsburgh. The Lions had a 27-23 fourth-quarter lead and the ball on the Steelers' 10-yard line. After three offensive plays failed to score a touchdown, the Lions lined up for a field goal attempt. It was a fake: holder Sam Martin took the snap and ran toward the end zone. But he fumbled along the way and the Steelers recovered on the 3-yard line. Their offense then drove 97 yards for the go-ahead touchdown and went on to win 37-27. It was a crushing loss for Detroit and one of a series of fourth-quarter collapses that season. They lost six of their last seven to end 7-9 and out of the playoffs.

Those two consecutive late-season collapses were Jim Schwartz's undoing. His temper didn't help either. He'd been involved in a post-game altercation with San Francisco Head Coach Jim Harbaugh after a game in 2011, threw an ill-timed challenge flag during the 2012 Thanksgiving game against Houston (see Chapter 10), and shouted expletives at booing fans during the final home game of 2013.[159] Schwartz was fired on December 30, 2013. His record as Lions' head coach was 29-51.

Jim Caldwell: Good Start, Then Mediocrity

The replacement was Jim Caldwell. The son of a Pentecostal minister, Caldwell was known for being level-headed and an excellent motivator. He'd spent seven years as an assistant in Indianapolis before taking over head coaching duties when Tony Dungy retired at the end of the 2008 season. Caldwell led the Colts to the Super Bowl in his first season (they lost to the Saints), but then Indianapolis went backward and Caldwell was fired after three seasons. He spent two years as an assistant in Baltimore before being hired by Detroit. Caldwell came to the Lions highly recommended: he was endorsed by Payton Manning, Tony Dungy, Bill Polian, and Ozzie Newsome.[160]

Caldwell is notable in Lions' history for being one of just a few head coaches to leave with a winning record. Unfortunately for Caldwell, his best season was his first season. After that the team slumped into mediocrity which is why he lasted just four years.

A few months after the Caldwell hiring, a major event in Lions' history took place. On March 9, 2014, longtime team owner William Clay Ford Sr passed away at the age of 88. Obituaries hailed him as being generous and well-liked, and also noted the Lions' lack of on-field success during his time as owner. Control of the team passed to his widow, Martha Firestone Ford.

Bill Ford would've been pleased with the Lions' performance during 2014. The team went 11-5 and qualified for the playoffs as a wild card. Caldwell and his coaches had put a significantly better team on the field: the offense was more balanced (60 percent pass/40 percent run) and the defense much improved. Draftees and free agents came together to form the league's 3rd ranked defense.[161] There was a solid line led by Ndamukong Suh and Ezekiel Ansah, quality linebackers including DeAndre Levy and Tahir Whitehead, and fast, aggressive defensive backs Darius Slay and Glover Quin. Detroit held opponents to 17.6 points per game which was a major improvement over the 23.5 points of the previous season.

The playoff game (described in the next chapter) took the Lions on the road to play the Eastern Division champion Dallas Cowboys. This contest was one of the most heartbreaking losses in recent Lions' history. Detroit looked invincible early on while building a 14-0 lead, and went to the locker room up 17-7 at halftime. The Cowboys staged a furious second-half comeback aided by several Lions' mistakes and a botched call by the officials. Dallas won 24-20.

The playoff loss haunted the Lions in 2015. They started the season 1-7 which included a memorable Monday night game in Seattle on October 5th. The Lions were down 10-13 late in the fourth quarter when Calvin Johnson appeared to be on his way to scoring a go-ahead touchdown. He was diving for the goal line when Seattle's Cam Chancellor knocked the ball out of his hands. The ball bounced into the end zone where the Seahawks' K.J. Wright swatted it over the back line. This illegal action by Wright should've given the Lions a first down on the 6-inch line, but instead the officials ruled it a touchback and Seattle's ball on the 20. It was another blown officials' call against the Lions and TV talking heads roundly condemned it. But the bottom line was another loss for the Lions.

After eight games and one victory, General Manager Martin Mayhew was fired. Lions-watchers thought Jim Caldwell would get the chop too, but he apparently saved his job when the Lions beat the Packers in Green Bay for the first time since 1991. However, the Packers turned the tables in their rematch in Detroit three weeks later. The Lions were once again victims of a bad referee call that cost them the game. Detroit seemed to have the game won when they stopped the Packers as time expired. But an official called a face-mask penalty on Lions' defensive lineman Devon Taylor. Replays showed that Taylor grabbed Packers' quarterback Aaron Rogers' shoulder pad, not his facemask. The phantom penalty gave the Packers one more play and they used it to complete a Hail Mary to tight end Richard Rogers in the end zone for a 27-23 win.

Detroit finished the year 7-9, the defense having dropped from 3rd in the league to 23rd by giving up 118 more points than in 2014. Calvin Johnson retired at the end of the season, another great player who toiled away on less-than-great Lions' teams. Johnson was inducted into the Professional Football Hall of Fame in 2021.

Bob Quinn (see below) was hired to be the general manager in 2016, and Caldwell returned to coach. The Lions qualified for the playoffs with a 9-7 record but were bounced in the first round by the Seattle Seahawks 6-26. The 2017 Lions produced another 9-7 season, but didn't qualify for the playoffs. The team had descended into mediocrity again which is why Caldwell was fired on January 1, 2018. His record with the Lions was 36-28.

Patriotitis

Every NFL fan knows that the New England Patriots are the great success story of the Super Bowl Era. The team reached the Super Bowl twice before winning their first championship at the end of the 2001 season. That title was the start of an incredible run that lasted about twenty years. Patriots have now played in eleven Super Bowls and won six. Other teams (the Packers, Bears, and Giants) have more NFL championships than the Patriots, but not during the Super Bowl Era.

In the NFL's highly competitive environment, less successful teams have long sought management and coaching talent from more successful teams. Recall that in 1957 Buddy Parker, the most accomplished head coach in Lions' history, quit the team before the season began. Two weeks later he was the head coach of the Pittsburgh Steelers. Back then Detroit was one of the best teams in the NFL and Pittsburgh one of the worst. Lesser-rans hiring talent from winners has been going on in the NFL since the early days.

During this century the Lions have been a bottom-tier team while New England has been top tier. We'd expect to see Detroit hiring talent from New England, and that's what happened in 2016 when the Lions appointed Bob Quinn as general manager. Quinn had been with the Patriots for sixteen years working in the area of player evaluation, rising from player personnel assistant to director of pro scouting. He'd been an integral part of a hugely successful organization so it's easy to understand why the Lions hired him. Then, after Jim Caldwell was fired, the Lions dipped deeper into the Patriots' pool by hiring Matt Patricia as head coach. Patricia had been on the Patriots' staff since 2004, his last six years as the team's defensive coordinator. Quinn, of course, was instrumental in making the hire.

Unfortunately for the Lions and their fans, the Quinn/Patricia pairing didn't work out. The Lions learned (as other teams have) that the Patriots' formula rarely extends beyond head coach Bill Belichick. Several NFL organizations have appointed former Patriots' front office staff and assistant coaches to higher positions and while a few have done well, most have not. Quinn and Patricia are examples of those who failed. Their record of player acquisition had hits and misses, and Patricia's overbearing demeanor didn't go over well in the locker room.

The New Era got off to a bad start in Patricia's first regular-season game as head coach. The 2018 opener was a Monday night game at Ford Field against the lowly New York Jets. The Lions jumped out to a 7-0 lead, but the Jets soon tied the game and led at halftime 17-10. The Lions tied the game in the third quarter but then it fell apart for Detroit. The Jets scored 31 points in the third quarter—four touchdowns and a field goal—and won a 48-17 blowout. That game set the tone for a season where the Lions never caught stride. They finished 6-10 and in last place in the NFC North. Critics said the Lions were predictable on offense and appeared lost on defense.

The 2019 season was even worse. The Lions had a new offensive coordinator and on opening day in Arizona jumped to a 17-3 halftime lead. They were ahead 24-6 in the fourth quarter when the Cardinals began a comeback. In the fourth quarter Detroit's offense appeared to have made a crucial first down to secure the win, but the play was nullified because (unbeknownst to the Lions on the field) Patricia called timeout just before the snap. Arizona scored 18 points and sent the game to overtime. The teams traded field goals in the extra period and the game ended in a tie. The Lions won their next two but then dropped twelve of thirteen and ended the season 3-12-1. The defense ranked 26th in points yielded and 31st in yards given up. Stafford missed half the season with a back injury—the most serious setback of his career. A gamer playing behind a weak offensive line, he was often injured.

The expectation heading into the 2020 season was that Patricia had to produce better results or he—and possibly Quinn as well—would be fired. It was another lost season. Incredibly, the Lions' 2020 defense was even worse than the 2008 version. The 2020 edition yielded 519 points and 6,716 yards of offense, both numbers among the worst in NFL history. The Lions kept blowing leads: 17 points to the Bears; 11 points to the Packers; 14 points to the Saints. The Lions were 4-5 when they traveled to Charlotte to play the 3-7 Carolina Panthers and lost 0-20. Four days later on Thanksgiving they hosted the 3-7 Houston Texans and were humiliated 25-41. Detroit couldn't do much of anything right in that game, at one point turning the ball over on three consecutive possessions. The defense was equally inept. It was an embarrassing loss on national television and the final straw for Quinn and Patricia.

The axe was wielded by Sheila Ford Hamp, daughter of Bill Sr and Martha Ford. Hamp, who'd taken control of the team in the summer of 2020, called a press conference two days after the Houston game to announce that Patricia and Quinn were fired. Darrell Bevell would serve out the season as interim head coach, and a search would be held for a new coach and general manager.[162] Sheila Ford Hamp explained that she liked Quinn and Patricia and wanted them to succeed, but "it clearly wasn't working."[163] No one was surprised by the firings, although most Lions watchers thought it would happen at the end of the season. Patricia left with a record of 13-29-1. The Lions had blown double-digit leads in nine of those losses and the tie in Arizona. *Detroit Free Press* sportswriter Shawn Windsor summarized Patricia's tenure this way: "The head coach struggled to communicate in the locker room, in the film room, and any room…and when he wasn't alienating his players, he was drawing up counterintuitive and baffling strategies."[164]

Yet Another New Beginning

The Lions made a fresh start in 2021 with a new general manager and head coach. General Manager Brad Holmes had been the Los Angeles Rams' director of college scouting and in charge of their college drafts from 2013-20. He has a solid reputation within the NFL for evaluating college talent. Head Coach Dan Campbell is a former NFL player who experienced the highest highs and the lowest lows. He was a tight end on the Lions from 2006-2008 which means he was a member of the winless 2008 team. At the opposite extreme, he played for two Super Bowls teams: the 2000 New York Giants (who lost to the Baltimore Ravens) and the 2009 New Orleans Saints (who defeated the Indianapolis Colts). Campbell went into coaching and served as an assistant in Miami and New Orleans. He was hired for his motivational skills and because ownership thought he could unite the team.[165]

Holmes and Campbell were considered high-risk hires. Holmes hadn't managed a team before, and Campbell never served as an NFL offensive or defensive coordinator which some consider a prerequisite for a head coaching position. Campbell did, however, serve as interim head coach of the Miami Dolphins during part of the 2015 season. By hiring Holmes and Campbell the Lions engaged in another outside-the-box experiment, although this one makes more sense than Matt Millen. When the announcement was made many fans and members of the media were understandably skeptical.[166] Given decades of Lions' futility, how could they not be?

One of Holmes's first moves was to trade Matthew Stafford to the Los Angeles Rams. The Lions were clearly in rebuild mode and Stafford was a proven veteran with major value on the players' market. The 2021 Rams were in a win-now mode whose moment has arrived. In exchange for Stafford the Rams gave up starting quarterback Jared Goff, their third-round pick in 2021, and first-round picks in 2022 and 2023. The trade appeared good for both teams: the Rams obtained a proven franchise quarterback who promptly took them to a Super Bowl win. The rebuilding Lions received three high-draft picks.

One encouraging item of note is that Holmes and Campbell used the Lions' first three draft picks in 2021 on linemen: Penei Sewell (OT), Levi Onwuzurike (DT), and Alim McNeill (DT). The third-round pick obtained from Los Angeles in the Stafford trade was used to select cornerback Ifeatu Melifonwu. The team's new leadership appears to understand how teams are built.

Campbell's first season as head coach was one of the Lions' most bizarre and frustrating campaigns in recent years. They finished the season 3-13-1, with five of the losses by a total of 13 points. It was a season of what-ifs. On opening day at Ford Field the Lions nearly executed a miracle comeback from a 17-41 deficit against San Francisco. Against Baltimore in the third game of the season the Lions once again fell victim to the longest field goal in NFL history as time expired. This time it was Justin Tucker kicking a 66-yarder that hit the crossbar and bounced through to win the game (details are in the next chapter). The Lions lost the fifth game of the season when the Vikings kicked a 54-yard field goal at the buzzer. On November 14th in Pittsburgh—where the Lions haven't won since 1955—the game went to overtime and turned into a comedy of errors as neither team seemed to want to win the game. It ended in a 16-16 tie. On November 21st the Lions lost by 3 points to Cleveland, then on Thanksgiving Day were defeated 14-16 when the Bears kicked a field goal at the end. So many heartbreaking losses, yet the Lions finally managed to turn it around on December 5th when they scored on an 11-yard touchdown pass to defeat the Vikings 29-27 on the final play of the game. It was their first victory of the season. Their other two victories were at home against Arizona and Green Bay.

The Lions 3-13-1 record in 2021 earned them the second pick in the 2022 draft which they used on defensive lineman Aidan Hutchinson from the University of Michigan. Hutchinson had an outstanding rookie season and along with other young talent helped the Lions improve to 9-8. The season started badly as the team was 1-6 at the end of October. But there was hope because four of the losses were by a total of 14 points. An especially heartbreaking defeat occurred in Minneapolis on September 25th when the Vikings scored a touchdown in the final seconds to win 28-24. The Lions then turned it around and went 8-2 over the remainder of the season with home wins against the Packers, Jaguars, Vikings, and Bears, and road wins against the Bear, Giants, Jets, and Packers. The season sweep of the Packers and Bears, combined with the split against the Vikings, put the Lions at 5-1 in the NFC North which was their best divisional performance in years. If the Lions could've secured one more victory they would have been in the playoffs and a team to be feared. Hopes are high heading into the 2023 campaign.

The Lions have been close to winning so many more games and have a coach and general manager who are building the team from the offensive and defensive lines outward. Has the tide finally turned in Detroit? Has the new generation of Ford family ownership hired a general manager and coach who can guide the team to sustained success? Or is this just another rebuilding program destined to end in disappointment?

Chapter 10
Some Lions' Lore

The Detroit Lions have been involved in their share of oddball events. Some have been humorous, some frustrating, some tragic. Taken together, they constitute Lions' lore. Here are a few notables that have taken place since the team's last championship in 1957.

The Paper Lion

At first glance, George Plimpton (1927-2003) seemed an unlikely character to become involved with the Detroit Lions. The son of an upper-class New York family, he grew up on Manhattan's Upper East Side and during his youth attended elite prep schools. After earning degrees from Harvard and Cambridge University in England, he began his career as a writer. In 1953 he became the first editor-in-chief of the *Paris Review* which is still a highly regarded literary magazine. He remained editor until his death in 2003. Plimpton was completely plugged into the literary world, and hobnobbed with prominent socialites, politicians, entertainers, athletes, and business tycoons. He was with Robert Kennedy in 1968 when Kennedy was shot in the Ambassador Hotel in Los Angeles. Plimpton helped subdue assassin Sirhan Sirhan who'd fired the fatal shots.

What made Plimpton different from many other elites was his willingness to get his hands dirty. He would try just about anything in pursuit of a story to write about. Plimpton was an advocate of "participatory journalism" which is the idea that if you're going to write about something, you should experience it first. Plimpton matched this journalistic concept with his enthusiasm for sports, and in an early project he pitched to major league baseball all-stars during an exhibition game. This experience was the material for his 1961 book *Out of My League*.

He decided to try football. His idea was to participate in a professional football team's training camp while trying out for "last-string quarterback." The real purpose was to gather material for a book. Over a four-year period he approached a number of NFL and AFL teams but couldn't find any willing to take him on. His luck finally changed when he met a director of the Detroit Lions (Plimpton did not say which one) who suggested he write to Lions' Head Coach George Wilson. Plimpton did so and to his surprise Wilson said yes.

The plan was for Plimpton to take part in the Lions 1963 training camp at Cranbrook Schools in Bloomfield Hills, Michigan while posing as a candidate for the Lions' third-string quarterback position. Plimpton, who was in his thirties at the time, knew the players wouldn't believe he was a fresh-faced rookie just out of college so he concocted a cover story: he was a ten-year veteran of the (fictional) cellar-dwelling Canadian semi-pro Newfoundland Newfs. His story turned out to be unnecessary because the Lions caught on to him quickly. Linebacker Wayne Walker had read *Out of My League* and knew who Plimpton was. Also, Plimpton clearly lacked NFL caliber football skills. And if anyone still hadn't figured it out, two weeks into training camp the *Detroit Free Press* reported that "rookie George Plimpton…is an author who has been in training camp with the Lions."[167] The players saw Plimpton as likeable and not a threat to take a position on the roster so they treated him as part of the gang.

The cooperative effort between Plimpton and the Lions turned out well for both parties.

Plimpton went through training camp wearing jersey #0 and wrote an entertaining, highly successful book about his experience. *Paper Lion: Confessions of a Last-String Quarterback* was published in 1966 and soon reached the best sellers' list. It sold around 100,000 hardback copies, and over 1 million when paperbacks are included. The book was a huge boon to Plimpton's writing career and good publicity for the Lions. It describes training camp, the players, the coaches, how they interacted, and includes many great stories. There's also interesting information about football: where else might you find a lengthy conversation where Hall of Famer Dick "Night Train" Lane explains the nuances of playing cornerback?

The book's success caught the attention of Hollywood. A producer was interested in making a movie, a scriptwriter was hired, and a director and actors lined up. Alan Alda was selected to play Plimpton; it was Alda's first starring role in a movie and eventually helped secure him the role of Hawkeye Pierce on the TV hit series *M*A*S*H*. Football players were needed, and the producer wanted the Lions to play themselves. Owner Bill Ford and GM Russ Thomas were persuaded to allow it to happen so the 1967 Lions' team went to Boca Raton, Florida where filming began in February 1968. It lasted six weeks and the players were paid from $350 to $1500 per week which was good offseason money back then.[168]

Joe Schmidt, who had just completed his first season as Lions' head coach, recalled the experience years later. "It was kind of fun to do but it was also a pain in the ass…I was worried about preparing game plans for the next season and I'm thinking what the hell is the season going to bring when we're jacking around in Florida. It took a long time to get the players' minds off the damn movie and concentrate on football. Everyone thought they would be movie stars."[169]

The movie *Paper Lion* (released in 1968) is loosely based on the book. Several players and coaches have prominent roles, and Plimpton makes a brief appearance playing owner Bill Ford. The movie was a financial success and helped launch the acting careers of not just Alda, but also Alex Karras who plays himself in the movie. Karras wasn't actually at the 1963 training camp with Plimpton because that was the year of his gambling suspension, but he was on the 1967 roster so he's in the movie. The producer was so impressed with Karras's performance that it led to a Hollywood screen test. Karras went on to have a successful acting career, perhaps best known for his role as Mongo the Neanderthal cowboy in *Blazing Saddles*.

As for Plimpton, he achieved enormous fame. He continued participatory journalism and tried an amazing array of activities. They included racing cars, sparring with a professional boxer, playing NHL hockey goalie, spending time on the pro golf tour, playing percussion instruments for the New York Philharmonic, trying his luck as a circus acrobat, and making brief appearances in several movies.[170] On September 21, 2003, the Lions brought him to Ford Field for a reunion of the 1967 team. Plimpton was there wearing his Lions' jersey #0. He and Alex Karras served as Lions' ceremonial captains and were at midfield for the pregame coin flip prior to the Lions/Vikings' game. Four days later Plimpton died of a heart attack at his home in New York.

Tom Dempsey's Foot

In the sports world, an athlete occasionally comes along and doesn't just break an existing record, they smash it. One famous example occurred during the 1968 Summer Olympics in Mexico City when US long-jumper Bob Beamon nailed a jump of 8.90 meters (29 feet, 2.40 inches). The previous record was 8.35 meters which means Beamon bested it by 0.55 meters, or nearly two feet. He went into physical shock when he realized what he'd done. His jump was 6.6 percent longer than the previous world record which in this context is an enormous difference. Beamon had pulled off an incredible athletic feat.[171]

Tom Dempsey (1947-2020), the placekicker for the New Orleans Saints, did something similar against the Lions on November 8, 1970. The scene was the old Tulane Stadium in New Orleans, Louisiana where the Detroit Lions were leading the Saints 17-16 with 0:02 left in the game. With the ball on their own 45-yard line, New Orleans had limited options to try to win. They decided to attempt a field goal because their placekicker had an exceptionally strong leg. A third-year player from California, Tom Dempsey was known for his booming kicks. He was also known for having accuracy issues.

The goal posts were located on the goal line in those days, so the line of scrimmage was 55-yards away. Normally, the holder sets the ball 7-yards behind the line of scrimmage which would've made the attempt 62-yards. But Saints' holder Joe Scarpati knew Dempsey would need an extra split second to launch such a big blast, so he told the kicker he was going to set the ball down 8-yards back. Scarpati also told the Saints' offensive linemen to hold their blocks longer than usual. In the heat of the moment Dempsey had no idea he was attempting a 63-yard field goal, nor that he was going for the record. He later said if he'd known all that, he might've missed.[172] The existing field goal record of 56 yards had been set in 1953 by the Baltimore Colts' Bill Rechichar.

Almost everything about Dempsey's record-setting field goal was improbable. For starters, Dempsey was born with no fingers on his right hand and no toes on his right (kicking) foot. He didn't let that stop him from playing sports in high school and college. A big, strong man, he was a lineman who became a kicker in an unlikely way. He was a member of the Palomar Junior College team in San Marcos, California and they needed a kicker. The coach had all his players line up and take turns kicking the ball, and since Dempsey's kicks went the furthest he became the place kicker.[173] After college, Dempsey tried out for the Packers as an offensive lineman but found the physical brutality of the NFL's trenches too much for his taste. He decided to focus on kicking instead and in 1968 landed a spot on the San Diego Chargers' reserve squad. It was Chargers' Head Coach Sid Gillman who had an orthopedist fit a special shoe for Dempsey to wear on his toeless foot. The shoe was squared-off on the front with 1.75 inches of leather inside. Dempsey was a straight-ahead kicker, not the soccer-style that is so common today.

Another reason why the field goal was improbable is because, from the Detroit Lions' point of view at least, the attempt never should've taken place. The Lions were heavy favorites going into the game. Detroit was 5-2 and would finish the season 10-4 and in the playoffs as the NFC's first wild card team. The Saints were 1-5-1, their head coach had been fired earlier in the week, and they were a league doormat on their way to a 2-11-1 season. New Orleans was in striking distance in the fourth quarter because the Lions had played badly. In a mistake-prone game for both teams, New Orleans took several key penalties and the Lions turned the ball over six times. Quarterback Bill Munson threw three interceptions, and there were three Lions' fumbles including two dropped punts by Nick Eddy. Detroit's defense kept the score low, but the Saints went ahead 16-14 in the fourth quarter. After receiving the kickoff, Lions' Head Coach Joe Schmidt sent Greg Landry into the game to quarterback. He'd seen enough of Munson.

The Lions' offense started on their 14-yard line and did a good job of moving the ball down the field while using up the clock. Eventually, the ball was on New Orleans' 18-yard line with 1:15 remaining. The Lions then executed three running plays, the final one being Mel Farr off left tackle. When that play was over, Landry called time-out. There was 0:17 left.

Landry had made a crucial mistake. It was fourth down and the Saints were out of time-outs. What Landry should've done was let the clock run down to just a few seconds so there was just enough time for the Lions to attempt a field goal. New Orleans wouldn't get the ball back, the final gun would sound, and—assuming the field goal was good—the Lions would head back to Detroit with the win.

Errol Mann executed the kick, an 18-yarder that put the Lions up 17-16. There was 0:11 left.

The Lions kicked off to the Saints. Their returner, Al Dodd ran out of bounds at the New Orleans 28. On the next play, quarterback Billy Kilmer threw a sideline pass to Dodd who made a great catch and went out of bounds at the 45. There was 0:02 left.

"Tell Stumpy to get ready to kick a long one," said Saints' assistant coach Don Heinrich. "Stumpy" was Dempsey's nickname on the team, and he liked it.

When Dempsey entered the game, the Lions laughed. They weren't laughing at Dempsey, they were laughing at the Saints for attempting such an implausible field goal. The Lions saw it as a last-ditch effort of grasping at straws by a losing team. Joe Schmidt was asked years later if he considered putting a tall player under the goalpost to try to block the kick. No, he said, because he didn't think it was a real attempt. The distance was too fantastic; he expected a trick play of some sort.[174]

The ball was snapped, Scarpati placed it, and Dempsey stepped forward. With a slight wind to his back he swung his big leg. There was a loud thump.

"It sounded like a cannon going off," said Lions' linebacker Wayne Walker.[175]

"It was an incredible kick," said Schmidt. "The ball went up to field goal height and sailed about 50-yards before coming down."[176] Observers with the angle said it cleared the crossbar by about one-foot. The two game officials standing near the goalpost raised their arms. Dempsey had kicked an NFL record-63-yard field goal and the Saints had won 19-17.

The crowd at Tulane Stadium went wild. The Lions stood in stunned disbelief while the Saints mobbed Dempsey and then carried him off the field on their shoulders. Tom Dempsey had beaten the record by an almost-unbelievable 7-yards. Bob Beamon beat the long-jump record by 6.6 percent; Tom Dempsey beat the field goal record by 13 percent.

While the losing Lions flew back to Detroit, the victorious Saints gathered in a bar in the French Quarter. They spent most of the night there partying. Dempsey's girlfriend—his future wife—said she didn't see him for days afterwards. He'd entered the annals of NFL history, setting a record that stood for forty-three years. Dempsey made the kick at an elevation of a few feet below sea level; when the record was finally broken in 2013 it was in the thin air of mile-high Denver, Colorado. His kicking shoe is on display in the Saints' Hall of Fame in New Orleans.[177] The Professional Football Hall of Fame in Canton, Ohio wanted it, but Dempsey insisted it stay in New Orleans.[178]

The Detroit Lions are entered in the record book as the victims of Tom Dempsey's amazing field goal.

The Sad Story of Chuck Hughes

Charles Frederick ("Chuck") Hughes (1943-1971) was a wide receiver and special teams' player for the Detroit Lions from 1970-1971. He grew up in Texas in a family with sixteen siblings (Chuck was number 11), and played college ball at Texas Western College (today's University of Texas - El Paso). He set several of the school's receiving records and was later inducted into their Athletic Hall of Fame. Drafted in 1967 by the Philadelphia Eagles, he was there for three seasons before being traded to the Lions in 1970. Hughes had a reputation for being a solid backup receiver and an excellent special teams' player.

Chuck Hughes has the sad distinction of being the only NFL player to die on the field during a game. Players have suffered paralyzing injuries, a few have died shortly after games, but only one expired during a game. It happened in the fourth quarter of a contest between the Lions and Bears at Tiger Stadium on October 24, 1971. In the final minutes, the Bears were ahead 28-23 and Detroit was trying to get the ball down the field to score a go-ahead touchdown. Lions' receiver Larry Walton had injured his ankle, so Hughes was in the game. The big play of the drive was a 32-yard pass from Greg Landry to Hughes who made a great catch before being tackled hard by two defenders on the Chicago 37-yard line. It was Hughes's first reception of the season. After the crunching blow he rose to his feet and trotted to the huddle. The Lions' medical doctors later said they believed that tackle was the event that caused Hughes's death a few minutes later.

On the next play, Landry threw out of bounds to stop the clock. That was followed by an incomplete pass to Charlie Sanders. On third down, Hughes lined up on the right side and went out for a pass. Landry threw to Sanders near the goal line, but the ball went off the tight end's hands. The clock stopped with 1:02 left. Hughes was near the 15-yard line when the play ended, and he turned and started toward the huddle. Bears' linebacker Dick Butkus (HOF) was watching Hughes and saw his eyes roll up. He clutched his chest and fell forward.

Butkus knew something was terribly wrong. He waved frantically toward the sideline and the Lions' doctors and trainers got the message: they sprinted onto the field toward Hughes. When they reached him, he wasn't breathing; they put him on his back, removed his helmet, and began CPR. A doctor attending the game, black leather bag in hand, climbed over the left-field wall and ran onto the field to help. The stadium went quiet as fans realized the gravity of the situation: Hughes was getting mouth-to-mouth resuscitation and chest massage while his face turned a horrid reddish-blue.

An ambulance parked outside the stadium was summoned. The doctors thought they'd gotten his heart restarted, but weren't sure. In the quiet of Tiger Stadium, fans could hear the siren as the ambulance sped away. He was taken to Henry Ford Hospital where doctors tried to save him, but to no avail. He was declared dead at 4:41 PM. "One dies officially when one is pronounced dead," said Dr. Edwin Guise, a Lions' team physician. "But in my heart, I feel Chuck died on the field."[179]

The contest between the Lions and Bears resumed a few minutes after the ambulance departed. They played out the last sixty-two seconds but were going through the motions. Except for a few clueless drunken fans, no one seemed to care that the Lions were unable to score.

The Lions retired to their locker room, closed it to the press, and waited for the news they all knew was coming. After the announcement came through, they filed out with sad faces and red eyes. A few minutes later owner Bill Ford emerged. "What can you say about a thing like this," he said in a halting voice. "It's unbelievable. Maybe on a racetrack you can see a thing like this happening, but this is simply inconceivable."[180]

An autopsy was performed the next day. The pathologist reported that Hughes had serious cardiovascular problems—there was a blood clot in one of his coronary arteries and evidence of a previous heart attack. Doctors believe the tackle after the 32-yard reception dislodged the clot which then blocked the blood flow to the heart. The previous heart attack had likely happened on September 4th. Hughes had collapsed after a preseason game and went to the hospital twice complaining of chest and stomach pain. He'd undergone tests but his cardiovascular problems went undetected. His wife later sued Henry Ford Hospital and received a settlement for an undisclosed sum.

The funeral took place in San Antonio, Texas on the Wednesday after the game. The entire Lions team attended. Chuck Hughes, 28 years old, was survived by his wife Sharon and their twenty-three months old son Shane.

Hughes's death knocked the stuffing out of the 1971 Lions. The team was 4-1 heading into the Chicago game but couldn't stay on-track afterwards. They finished 7-6-1, in second place in the Central, and out of the playoffs. Joe Schmidt considered the tragedy a major reason for his team's underperformance that year. Several Chicago Bears believed the same was true for their team.

The Lions established a scholarship fund for Hughes's son, and each year the team presents the Chuck Hughes Award "to the player who, because of hard work and determination, showed significant development and improvement during the past year."[181] Thirty-four years passed before another Lion wore Hughes's #85.

Fifty years after the terrible event, Joe Schmidt reminisced about Hughes: "Chuck didn't have great speed, but he was a good player, a great guy and teammate, and he worked like hell at practice. He would follow me up and down the sidelines asking to get in the game but Chuck never complained."[182]

The NFL's Shortest Overtime Game

On Thanksgiving Day 1980, the Lions once again managed to get themselves in the record books for losing in a notable way. This time they gave up a kick return for a touchdown on the first play of a sudden-death overtime period. The Lions lost the shortest overtime contest in NFL history.

The game was yet another case of the Lions blowing a fourth-quarter lead. They were ahead of the Chicago Bears 17-3 at the end of three quarters, and looked to be in control of the game. Then the Bears staged a comeback, putting together fourth-quarter touchdown drives of 86 and 94 yards. The second touchdown occurred when Chicago's quarterback Vince Evans ran into the end zone as time expired, and the extra point tied the game. The Lions' defense, offense, and special teams all failed near the end. Twice in the fourth quarter the Bears stopped the Lions' offense on third-and-1 plays. With the score tied 17-17, the game went into sudden-death overtime.

Regular-season overtime games were relatively new in the NFL at the time. Overtime rules had long existed for playoff games, but weren't established for the regular season until 1974. The league changed various rules that year to make games more exciting; in addition to overtime, they moved the goalposts to the back of the end zone and restricted the ability of pass defenders to hit receivers down the field.[183] The overtime period would last 15:00 unless either team scored in which case the game was over. If the teams were still even at the end of the period, then the game was a tie. During the five NFL seasons prior to the rule change (1969-1973), there were thirty-four tie games, and during the five years after (1974-1978) there were three.

The 1980 Lions/Bears' game was only the second overtime experience for the Lions (in 1975 they lost to the Chiefs). At the start of overtime, the referee flipped the coin and the Bears (the visiting team calls coin flips) said tails. The coin landed tails up and Chicago chose to receive the ball. The teams lined up for the kickoff and the Lions' Eddie Murray launched the ball toward the Chicago goal line. Bears' running back Dave Williams caught it on the 5-yard line.

Williams ran forward between blockers for about twenty yards, then veered to his left. He angled toward the sideline, reaching it at about the Lions' 30 while outsprinting would-be tacklers along the way. When he reached the end zone the Bears won 23-17 and the huge crowd at the Silverdome booed. Afterwards, Lions' special teams' players blamed themselves for overcommitting to the middle of the field on the play.[184]

It was a devastating loss for the Lions, and eventually cost them the NFC Central Division title. After the game, Coach Monte Clark said, "It was probably the most disappointing, bitter loss I've ever experienced."[185] (This was three years before Eddie Murray missed wide-right in San Francisco.)

According to the official record of the game the kickoff return took 21 seconds. However, that number is not accurate. NFL rules specify that the game clock begins moving when a player on the return team touches the ball. It was the opening kickoff of the overtime period, so when Williams caught the ball there was 15:00 on the clock. He then ran at top speed toward the goal line 95 yards away, crossing about three-fourths of the width of the field on the way. In other words, Williams ran roughly 120 yards to score the touchdown. There's no way an NFL running back going top-speed needs 21 seconds to cover 120 yards. The official in charge of the game clock must have dozed off or lost track of time-keeping during the excitement. Watching a replay of the kick return and using a stopwatch, the play took 12-13 seconds.

By either measure, it was by far the shortest overtime game played up to that time. The previous record had been set in 1979 when it took 1:41 of overtime play for the Tampa Bay Buccaneers to defeat the Baltimore Colts. The Lions/Bears' overtime game cut that time by 1:20.

The 0:21 overtime game held the record for seventeen years, and it likely would've been much longer had Williams' kick return been properly timed. In 1997 the New Orleans Saints used 0:17 to defeat the Seattle Seahawks. The sudden-death period in that game consisted of a kickoff into the end zone (no time expired), a pass interception (the clock stops on a change of possession), and a field goal. In 2001 Chicago defeated San Francisco in 0:16 (kickoff followed by pick-six interception). Then, in 2002, the only other overtime game to end on a kickoff return took place: the New York Jets ran back the opening kick against the Buffalo Bills. The 96-yard return took 0:14 which suggests how bad the timekeeping was in the Lions/Bears' 1980 game.

The current record, set in a January 2012 playoff game, is 0:11. This time will be hard to beat. It happened in a wild card game in Denver between the Steelers and Broncos. The Steelers kicked off to start the overtime period, and the ball went through the end zone for a touchback. Thus, there was 15:00 on the clock when the Broncos lined up for their first offensive play. Quarterback Tim Tebow dropped back to pass and threw to Demaryius Thomas who caught it on the 38 and streaked to the end zone for the game-winning touchdown.[186]

Lions Take the Wind

On the afternoon of Sunday, November 24, 2002, in Champaign, Illinois, the wind was blowing out of the north at 17 miles per hour. That's a relevant piece of information because the Detroit Lions were there that day playing the Chicago Bears. Soldier Field in Chicago, the Bears' regular home stadium, was being rehabbed so the Bears were playing their 2002 home schedule at the University of Illinois' stadium 130 miles to the south.

The wind played a pivotal role because it led Detroit's Head Coach Marty Mornhinweg to make a decision that attracted national attention, may have cost the Lions the game, and was instrumental in getting him fired at the end of the season. Rarely in modern NFL history has such an inconsequential game in terms of the standings received so much publicity.

The Lions were in the early stages of the Matt Millen Era. Marty Mornhinweg, the first head coach Millen hired, was in his second (and final) year. Detroit had yet to win a road game under Mornhinweg's leadership, and the team was 3-7 in 2002. The 2-8 Bears were having a similarly dismal season; after starting 2-0 they'd lost eight straight. The only thing the Lions and Bears were contending for in 2002 was the higher draft pick when the season was over.

It's yet another story of the Lions blowing a lead and then losing on a play that never should've happened. They were ahead 17-7 with 3 minutes remaining in the fourth quarter when the game began to unravel. The Bears took possession on Detroit's 9-yard line and moved the ball down the field in twelve plays. Their touchdown came on a 23-yard pass from Jim Miller to Dez White, and the extra point made the score Detroit 17, Chicago 14.

The Lions received the kickoff and needed to drain the clock to win. But they couldn't do it because two offensive holding penalties stopped the clock and moved them backwards. The offense went three-and-out and Detroit punted. The wind shortened John Jett's kick and the Bears started on the Lions' 47. Chicago moved forward, then backward, and Detroit's defense stiffened enough to force the Bears into a fourth-and-twenty on the Lions' 45. Quarterback Jim Miller took the snap and fell down, but then rose to his feet and completed a 33-yard pass to White who was down on the Lions' 12-yard line. Four plays later, Bears' placekicker Paul Edinger tied the score 17-17 by hitting a 22-yard field goal as time expired.

Now the really bad comedy began.

During the short break prior to the overtime period, Edinger dashed out onto the field and tried a few 40-yard field goals into the wind. They barely cleared the crossbars. Apparently, the Lions' coaches didn't notice.

The team captains gathered at midfield for the coinflip which the Lions won. They had the option to receive the kick or choose which end zone to defend.

Football wisdom says: win the flip, take the ball. The overtime rules in place at the time were that the team that scored first won the game. Furthermore, since 1994 when kickoffs were moved from the 35 to the 30-yard line, the team that had won the overtime coin flip (almost all of them chose to receive the kick) had won 60 percent of the games.[187] However, Mornhinweg told his captains to defend the north end zone so the Lions would have the wind at their backs. The Bears would get the ball.

It was a strange decision, but not unprecedented. In the 326 regular-season overtime games in the NFL up to that time, the team that won the coinflip had chosen an end of the field to defend eight times.[188] Mornhinweg's plan, of course, was that the Lions' defense would stop the Bears, and then Detroit's offense could get into position to kick a field goal aided by the wind. However, the decision went against the statistical odds. Furthermore, it meant the Lions were relying on their defense which had failed in the fourth quarter. They'd given up two scoring drives, allowed the Bears to convert a fourth-and-20 play, and lost a 10-point lead. They were also tired: they'd been on the field for 8½ of the last 10 minutes.

The Bears' captains were flabbergasted by the Lions' decision. "I told their captains, Y'all are stupid," said safety Larry Whigham. "That's dumb. And they didn't say anything to me. I mean, come on! I don't know what their coaches were thinking about."[189]

"I couldn't believe it," said linebacker Brian Urlacher. "I'm glad they did, obviously, but I couldn't believe it."[190]

Mornhinweg's decision had an unintended consequence as well: it insulted the Bears' offense. "We took it personally," said center Olin Kreutz. "They're telling us their defense is going to shove the ball down our throats and that got guys angry and wanting to prove something to everybody."[191]

The Bears fielded the kickoff 2 yards behind the goal line and returned it to their 35. The offense was then able to move the ball across midfield to the Lions' 35-yard line. On a third-and-8 play, Miller threw an incomplete pass and a penalty flag appeared: offensive holding against the Bears.

Mornhinweg now faced another decision: (1) accept the penalty and move the Bears back to the Lions' 45 where they would have a third-and-18, or (2) decline the penalty which would leave the ball on the Lions' 35 with the Bears facing fourth-and-8. A field goal attempt from there would be 52-yards into the wind, and Edinger had barely made 40-yarders during the break before overtime. The Bears, knowing Edinger couldn't hit a 52-yarder and thinking the Lions would refuse the penalty, sent their punter onto the field.

Mornhinweg, who was having a bad day, must not have seen the punter because he accepted the penalty. The Bears were moved back 10-yards. They faced third-and-18.

"I wanted them to have no or little opportunity to make a field goal, so I backed them up," said Mornhinweg after the game. "And again I had confidence in our defense to go in and make a play."[192]

His confidence was misplaced. Miller threw a 15-yard completion which moved the ball to the Detroit 30. It was fourth-and-3 and still too far to try a field goal. Miller then threw 5-yards to White for a first down that never should've occurred. That was followed by three straight running plays that moved the ball to the Detroit 22. Edinger came out to attempt a 40-yarder, and when the kick went through the uprights the Bears won 20-17. They hoisted Edinger onto their shoulders and carried him off the field.

Afterwards, Mornhinweg was asked about his decision to let the Bears have the ball at the start of overtime. "I would do that again," he said. "Well, knowing the outcome of this game, I wouldn't, but if it were a similar situation, I would do that again."[193]

Not surprisingly, Lions' fans were apoplectic after the loss. The Detroit media raked Mornhinweg over the coals.[194] The Lions' players were angry but none of them criticized the coach in public. The loss made Mornhinweg's record as Lion's head coach 5-22 and the coinflip decision helped seal his fate. The team lost the rest of their games in 2002, and never did win a road game during Mornhinweg's two years as coach. When he was fired at the end of the season Matt Millen cited the Bears' game as one of the reasons.

The Calvin Johnson Rule

Some of the NFL's rules have been written to address unusual situations that involved various players and coaches. Those persons' names aren't in the NFL's official rulebook, but it's widely known that the rules exist because of something they did.

The Bronco Nagurski Rule is a famous example. In the early 1930s, a forward pass had to originate from at least 5-yards behind the line of scrimmage. This rule came to the forefront during the 1932 NFL Championship Game between the Bears and Portsmouth Spartans (the future Detroit Lions).[195] In the fourth quarter of a scoreless game, Bronco Nagurski—a fearsome two-way player for the Bears—was the ballcarrier and started toward the line of scrimmage, then stopped and threw a pass over the heads of the Spartans' linemen who were massing to tackle him. Red Grange caught the pass for the game-winning touchdown. A major argument ensured when Spartans' coach Potsy Clark claimed that Nagurski's pass was illegal because it was thrown within 5 yards of the line of scrimmage. Clark lost the argument and the Spartans lost the game, but in 1933 the NFL instituted the Bronco Nagurski Rule which allows a forward pass from anywhere behind the line of scrimmage.

Many other famous examples exist. The Tom Dempsey rule specifies that a kicker's shoe must conform to that of a normal shoe. The Ricky Williams Rule says that a player's hair is part of their uniform, thus defenders can grab the ball carrier's hair while tackling him. The Emmitt Smith Rule penalizes a player for removing his helmet on the field of play. The Bill Belichick Rule allows one defensive player on the field to have a speaker in his helmet so he can receive instructions from the bench.[196]

There's also a Calvin Johnson Rule. This one exists because of a controversial play that occurred near the end of the Lions/Bears' contest in Chicago on opening day of the 2010 season. The Lions—who'd won a total of two games during 2008-09—were hoping for better things in 2010. They were off to a good start that afternoon and led 14-10 near the end of the first half thanks to two touchdown runs by their rookie running back Jahvid Best. Unfortunately for Detroit, with 0:29 remaining in the half Bears' defensive end Junius Peppers sacked Matthew Stafford who landed on his right shoulder and fumbled the ball. Stafford left the field and would play in just two more games that season before having surgery. The Bears recovered the fumble and kicked a field goal before halftime to make the score Detroit 14, Chicago 13.

Shaun Hill came in to play quarterback for Detroit. The score remained 14-13 until late in the fourth quarter when the Bears scored a touchdown to take a 19-14 lead (their 2-point attempt failed).

The Lions received the kickoff and started on their own 17. They had one timeout and there was 1:27 remaining. Hill suddenly got hot and completed four passes in a row which moved the ball to the Chicago 25. On the next play Hill spiked the ball to stop the clock. The Lions faced second-and-10 with 0:31 remaining.

The play of the game came next. Calvin Johnson, the Lions' go-to receiver, split out on the right side. At the snap he ran toward the end zone covered by Chicago defensive back Zachary Bowman. Quarterback Hill dropped back and threw to Johnson in the end zone. Johnson outjumped Bowman and secured the ball in his enormous hands. While Johnson's feet were returning to earth, Bowman fell against him which caused Johnson's body to tilt backwards. His right foot touched the ground first, then his left, and he fell. On his way down he transferred the ball to his right hand and used his left hand to break the fall. He landed on his rear end with his knee touching the ground, and then his right hand (which held the ball) headed toward the turf. The ball hit the ground and separated from his hand. The official standing a few feet away raised his arms: touchdown.

The Lions bench erupted. The crowd at Soldier Field let out a collective groan.

"I thought the game was over," said Johnson. "The first thing that went through my head was 'We won. We finally beat the Bears.' And I come to find out after I was sprinting halfway across the field that it was something else."[197]

The Lions stopped celebrating when they realized the game officials were huddling. There was a delay while the play was reviewed. Then the announcement: incomplete pass.

Johnson was sure he'd scored. "I figured that if I got two feet and a knee down, to me it's a catch."[198]

Coach Jim Schwartz argued, but to no avail. The play looked like a catch, and the Lions thought it was a catch as did many fans at Soldier Field. Johnson had possession of the ball, two feet on the ground, and then a knee on the ground. The problem was losing his grip on the ball when it hit the ground. According to the rules, Johnson had not completed the catch.

Had Johnson remained on his feet it would've been ruled a catch. However, the Chicago defender prevented that from happening when he fell against Johnson and caused him to lose his balance. Johnson had to maintain possession of the ball when he hit the ground. The referee, Gene Steratore, said: "[I]n order for the catch to be completed he has got to maintain possession of the ball through the entire process of the catch."[199] Jim Schwartz later agreed that the ruling was correct. The Lions didn't file a protest.

The incident set off a media storm and most every TV sports talking head weighed in. Two of the most respected in the business disagreed. Former receiver Cris Collinsworth said, "It has been pounded into our heads, time after time, that if you make a catch and there is contact…you have to maintain complete possession over that ball, all the way to the ground…I thought they got it right." Former NFL coach Tony Dungy thought different. "That's a catch…Cris Collinsworth thinks it's an incomplete pass, but that's a catch."[200]

Following the controversial play, the Lions tried two more passes into the end zone but both were incomplete. The Bears' offense took over on downs, their quarterback took a knee, and the game was over. It was another heartbreaking loss for the Lions who moments before thought they'd done something wonderful: pulled off an opening day come-from-behind victory on the road against a division rival. Instead, they left the field crushed. The Lions went on to finish the 2010 season 6-10 and in third place in the NFC North.

The non-catch led the NFL to adopt the Calvin Johnson Rule. It wasn't a new rule *per se*, instead it clarified an existing rule about the definition of a catch. Here it is:

> *If a player goes to the ground in the act of catching a pass (with or without contact by an opponent), he must maintain control of the ball after he touches the ground, whether in the field of play of the end zone. If he loses control of the ball, and the ball touches the ground before he regains control, the pass is incomplete. If he regains control prior to the ball touching the ground, the pass is complete.*

Coach's Challenge Goes Bad

Each year on Thanksgiving Day the professional football spotlight shines on Detroit. The Lions have been hosting a game on the holiday since 1934, and for decades it's been the only NFL game on television during its afternoon time slot.[201] The games receive an exceptional amount of attention: the 2021 contest between the Lions and Bears drew 26.75 million television viewers.

Since the Detroit Lions are involved, the contests have had their share of oddball moments. The quick overtime loss to the Bears in 1980 happened on Thanksgiving Day. The famous "coinflip game" against the Pittsburgh Steelers took place on Thanksgiving in 1998. That was the affair when during the coinflip before overtime Steelers' captain Jerome Bettis said "Hea-tails" while the coin was in the air. Bettis meant to say "tails", but the referee interpreted his response as "heads." The coin came up tails, so the Lions were awarded the toss and chose to receive the kick. They promptly moved the ball down the field and kicked a field goal to win the game. The messy coinflip led the NFL to institute the Jerome Bettis Rule four days later which says the visiting team calls the toss *before the coin is flipped*, not while the coin is in the air.

Another famous Thanksgiving game took place in 2012. The Lions came out on the short end of this one and what made it truly exceptional is that their head coach, Jim Schwartz, made a foolish mistake that likely cost the Lions the game. A breathtaking sequence of events occurred in the third quarter that would've turned out fine for the Lions if Schwartz had just taken a moment to think before acting.

The Lions' opponents that day were the Houston Texans. An up-and-coming AFC team at the time, they'd gone 10-6 the previous season and reached the divisional round of the playoffs. They arrived in Detroit in 2012 with a 9-1 record and on the short list of Super Bowl contenders. The Lions were 4-6 and hoping to salvage what looked to be another lost season.

The Lions had a good first half and led 21-14 at the break. They carried their success into the third quarter by kicking a field goal to extend their lead to 24-14. An upset seemed possible.

Detroit kicked off after the field goal and Houston started on their own 19. A deep pass down the middle fell incomplete. On second down they handed off to running back Justin Forsett who ran up the middle and gained 7-yards before being tackled on the 26 by Lions' defensive backs Erik Coleman and Louis Delmas. Forsett's elbow and knee touched the turf, but he rose to his feet and continued running toward the end zone. Believing Forsett was down, the Lions' defenders watched him go, except for defensive lineman Lawrence Jackson who gave chase but couldn't catch up. No whistle sounded, and an official followed Forsett down the field. When the ball crossed the goal line the official signaled touchdown.

The officials had botched the call by not blowing the play dead on the 26. Should the Lions have tackled Forsett again? Not if they thought the play was over because they would've been open to a personal foul penalty for a late hit. Had the sequence ended there it would've turned out fine for the Lions because all touchdowns are subject to review. Replays clearly showed Forsett down on the 26. The ball would've been spotted there with the Texans facing third and 3.

But Jim Schwartz messed everything up by throwing a challenge flag.

"Yeah, I know the rule," Schwartz said afterwards. "You can't challenge a turnover or a scoring play and I overreacted. I was so mad that they didn't call [Forsett] down 'cause he was obviously down on the field. I had the flag out of my pocket before he ever scored the touchdown."[202]

Schwartz had made a major mistake. Throwing the flag was a penalty: unsportsmanlike conduct for throwing a challenge flag when prohibited from doing so. Under the rules at the time, the penalty obligated the officials to cancel the automatic review and have the original call (touchdown) stand.

"That's all my fault," said Schwartz. "I overreacted in that situation and I cost us a touchdown."[203]

Thus, the Texans were credited with an 81-yard touchdown run and to add insult to injury the Lions were penalized 15 yards on the ensuing kickoff. The officials had made a mistake and Schwartz compounded it. The crowd at Ford Field was in an uproar. Ironically, Schwartz had been in a postgame altercation with San Francisco's coach Jim Harbaugh the year before when Schwartz got on Harbaugh's case for throwing a challenge flag in a similar situation.

The phantom touchdown and successful PAT put the Texans 3 points down. Later that quarter Houston tied the game with a field goal. During the fourth quarter the teams traded touchdowns. The score was 31-31 at the end of regulation.

Both teams missed field goals during the overtime period. The Texans failed from 51 yards, and Detroit's Jason Hanson hit the right upright from 47 yards. Houston finally kicked the game winner with 2:25 remaining to defeat the Lions 34-31.

It was another what-if game for Detroit. If not for their head coach's braindead moment they might've pulled off a major upset. Instead, they suffered their third loss in a row and their ninth consecutive Thanksgiving Day defeat. The Lions didn't win another game that year and finished 4-12. Schwartz returned to coach in 2013 but was fired at the end of the season.

Fans watching the 2012 Thanksgiving game realized there was a flaw in the NFL's rulebook. Sportswriter Jeff Seidel summarized it this way: "a play that should have been reviewed, but it wasn't reviewed, because Schwartz asked for it to be reviewed."[204] The NFL fixed the problem in March 2013 by instituting the Jim Schwartz Rule: a team is penalized if its coach throws a challenge flag in a situation where an automatic review is warranted, but the review proceeds and the call on the field can be overturned.

The Call/No Call in Dallas

For fans of the Detroit Lions, few games have been more painful to watch than the 20-24 playoff loss to the Dallas Cowboys on January 4, 2015. In one single game all of the elements that have prevented the Lions from achieving success over the decades were on display: taking an early lead and then having it slip away, quality players choking at key moments, turnovers at the worst possible times, and a critical referee call going against them. All of those things happened that day, and when it was over Lions were weeping in the locker room in Texas. Many fans surely were doing the same thing in their homes in Michigan.

In the eyes of many, the 2014 Lions were the franchise's best entry since 1991. Issues on the offensive line hindered point production, but the defense was outstanding. Ranked 3rd in points allowed and 2nd in yards given up, they made Detroit a playoff team to be taken seriously. Unfortunately, the Lions lost a chance to win the North because they played badly in Green Bay in the last game of the season. The Packers' 30-20 victory made them division champs and Detroit a wild card. If the game had gone the other way, the Lions would've had a playoff bye week and then hosted a divisional game.

Instead, they went on the road to Dallas for a first-round game as a wild card. The Cowboys were 6.5-point favorites but many thought Detroit had a chance. If their quarterback Matthew Stafford could put together a good game, if the receivers caught the passes, and if the defense played to its potential then Detroit could win.

The Lions started the game as world-beaters. In the first quarter Matthew Stafford hit Golden Tate for a 51-yard touchdown, then running back Reggie Bush went outside left tackle and scored from 18-yards out. The Lions led 14-0 after one quarter. During the second quarter the Lions gave up one bad play: a 76-yard TD pass from Tony Romo to Terrance Williams. Two Lions' defenders missed a chance to tackle Williams on his way to the end zone. Detroit partially atoned by kicking a field goal in the final seconds and went into the locker room ahead 17-7. The defense had allowed Dallas 30 yards rushing and held star receiver Dez Bryant to one catch for 2 yards.

However, there was still a half to play and Lions' fans know how that can turn out. Detroit received the opening kickoff, and on first down Matthew Stafford dropped back to pass. His throw was deflected by a defensive lineman and landed in the hands of a linebacker. The Cowboys didn't score off the interception, but it was a harbinger of things to come. The Lions' only points of the half came midway in the third quarter when Matt Prater kicked a 37-yard field goal. The Lions led 20-7.

After that it was all Dallas. Demarco Murray ran in from the 1-yard line at 2:54 of the third quarter, then at 12:16 of the fourth Dallas kicked a field goal to draw within 3.

The killer sequence began with 8:25 left in the game. The Lions faced third-and-1 on the Dallas 46. Stafford dropped back to pass and threw to Brandon Pettigrew who was 17 yards downfield between the left hashmarks and sideline. Pettigrew was covered by Anthony Hitchens who grabbed the receiver's jersey, let go, and then with his back to the ball prevented Pettigrew from making the catch. The pass was incomplete and a yellow penalty flag hit the field. The crowd in Dallas groaned.

Referee Pete Morelli announced pass interference against Dallas and moved the ball to the spot of the foul. First down Lions on the Dallas 29, or so it appeared.

But no! The officials met and discussed, and a moment later the flag was picked up and the ball moved back to the original line of scrimmage. The referee announced there was no foul, but it happened so quickly the TV cameras missed it.

The Lions went berserk. Even for a team that has had some screwy things happen to them over the years, this was new territory. A penalty flag is thrown, the penalty is announced, the penalty is marked off, and then the penalty is cancelled. Had anyone seen that before? Stafford, who was wearing a microphone during the game kept shouting "Unbelievable!" at the referee.

Afterwards, the official explanation from the NFL was that the back judge called the interference penalty, but the head linesman, who supposedly had the better view, said, "the contact was minimal and didn't warrant pass interference."[205] The pass interference call may have been a matter of judgement, but Hitchens grabbing Pettigrew's jersey wasn't. The officials missed it. The NFL's head official, Dean Blandino, later said that Hitchens got away with defensive holding.[206] At a minimum it should've been first down Lions on the Dallas 41.

When play resumed the Lions faced fourth-and-1. They took a delay-of-game penalty and then punter Sam Martin choked at a very bad moment: his kick went 10 yards beyond the line of scrimmage. The Cowboys took possession on their 41 and after that Lions' fans watched helplessly while their team gave the game away. Dallas moved down the field aided by two Detroit defensive holding penalties, at one point executing a fourth-and-6 play. Dallas scored the go-ahead touchdown on an 8-yard pass from Romo to Williams. The Lions had one more possession, but an offensive lineman was beaten and Stafford was sacked and fumbled the ball away. The Lions' offense, which had scored 17 points in the first half, scored 3 in the second half. The defense, which gave up one bad play in the first half, allowed the Cowboys to score touchdown-field goal-touchdown on their last three possessions. The final score was Dallas 24, Detroit 20.

"The first half, we were playing pretty well," said coach Jim Caldwell. "But we just couldn't sustain it."[207]

Mitch Albom summarized the game as follows: "The best Lions' season in decades ends the way the last seven postseasons have ended. One-and-out. One maddening, seducing, frustrating, teeth-gnashing, tear-inducing one-and-out."[208]

Not Again!

The scene: the Detroit Lions have kicked a fourth-quarter field goal to take a 17-16 lead. With little time left on the game clock they're in a strong position to win. The kickoff puts their opponents deep in their own end. It will take a football miracle to win.

Yet somehow in the waning moments yards are gained, enough to try an implausibly-long desperation field goal attempt as time expires. The kick—if good—will set the record for the longest field goal in NFL history. It will also defeat Detroit 19-17.

Lions' fans old enough to remember think: *Haven't I seen this movie before? In 1970? Tulane Stadium? The New Orleans Saints? Tom Dempsey?*

*Is this a **deju vu**?*

Incredibly, what occurred on November 8, 1970, happened again on September 26, 2021. The recent version wasn't at Tulane Stadium in New Orleans, it was at Ford Field in Detroit. The Lions' opponents weren't the New Orleans Saints, they were the Baltimore Ravens. The kicker wasn't Tom Dempsey going for a 63-yarder, it was Justin Tucker trying 66-yards. And yes, both times it ended badly for the Lions.

Tom Dempsey's 63-yarder in 1970 set the NFL field goal distance record that lasted for forty-three years. It was tied five times before finally being broken in Denver on December 8, 2013, by the Bronco's Matt Praeter (a future Lion). He kicked a 64-yarder just before halftime against the Tennessee Titans. Praeter's record stood for nearly eight years until Justin Tucker kicked his 66-yarder in Detroit.

Tucker's field goal occurred at the end of the third game of Dan Campbell's tenure as Lions' head coach. Detroit was seeking their first win of the season while the Ravens were 1-1 and coming off a victory over the defending AFC Champion Kansas City Chiefs. Baltimore dominated Detroit, but the score was close enough for the Lions to mount a comeback because Raven's receivers had dropped several passes thrown by their quarterback Lamar Jackson. When Tucker kicked a 37-yard field goal with 0:41 left in the third quarter Baltimore was ahead 16-7.

The Lions made a game of it in the fourth quarter. They scored a touchdown with 8:16 left, and on their next possession worked the ball down the field deep into the Ravens' end. With a first down on the 14-yard line and 2:00 left, Detroit executed the first of three running plays. Campbell's plan was to run down the clock, force the Ravens to burn their timeouts, and if the Lions didn't make a first down, kick the go-ahead field goal. Baltimore would get the ball back with little time remaining.

On the third-down play, Lions' running back Jamaal Williams was stopped on the 17-yard line. Ryan Santoso came in and kicked a 34-yarder that put Detroit ahead 17-16. There was 1:04 left and the Ravens were out of timeouts.

The Ravens started on their 25. On the first play, the Lions sacked Jackson for a 3-yard loss. With the clock running, Baltimore hurried to the line and ran a play that was an incomplete pass. On third down the Lions' pass rushers nearly sacked Jackson before chasing him out of bounds on the 16. The clock stopped with 0:26 left. The Ravens faced fourth-and-19. Lions' coach Dan Campbell called timeout to decide what defensive play to run.

The clock stoppage turned out to be a mistake. "It helped because Coach changed the play," Lamar Jackson said after the game. "He went to another play and that's what helped us get that field goal drive going. I was happy for that timeout because we needed a breather. Our linemen needed a breather."[209]

The Lions decided to rush three. The Ravens' offensive coordinator called for a pass to Sammy Watkins down the left side of the field. The ball was snapped and Jackson had plenty of time to set up and complete the pass to Watkins who was tackled on the Lions' 48. First down, and the clock was moving. The Ravens' rushed to the line and executed the spike-play. There was 0:07 left.

The Ravens lined up for another play. The plan was to throw a quick sideline route to get the ball closer for a field goal attempt. They set up and the play clock expired before the ball was snapped. The gap was later estimated to be 1.8 seconds.[210] For some reason the officials didn't call a penalty; there should've been a delay-of-game costing Baltimore 5-yards which likely would've put them into Hail Mary territory instead of the field goal attempt. Play continued: the ball was snapped and finding no one open, Jackson threw it out of bounds. The clock read 0:03.

Tucker entered the game to try the field goal. Like Dempsey's attempt in 1970, the holder set up 8-yards behind the line of scrimmage. It was an unlikely kick but not impossible for Tucker. A baritone opera singer in his spare time, he ranks as one of the best kickers in NFL history and has routinely hit field goals of 50-plus yards. He was also on an incredible hot streak: he'd made forty-nine straight fourth-quarter and overtime field goals dating to the 2016 season. Lions' fans remember his career day at Ford Field in 2013 when he kicked six field goals (including a 61-yarder) to account for all the Ravens' points in an 18-16 victory over Detroit.

The ball was snapped, the holder placed it. Tucker approached it like a kickoff, launching the ball and then landing on his kicking foot. It was a technique he'd been working on because he saw himself "becoming more and more of a dinosaur in this league at 31-years old."[211] The ball sailed toward the goal posts; it would be close. The crowd yelled their approval when it hit the crossbar and bounced high into the air spinning end over end. It looked to be just short. But the fans' shouts of joy turned to groans of agony when the ball landed on the turf behind the goalpost. The officials raised their arms.

It had happened again. The Lions had lost 19-17 on a last second, record-breaking field goal.

Chapter 11
Strategies Moving Forward

Lions' fans want the current rebuilding program to achieve success, but suppose it ends up in failure like all the other attempts of the last six-plus decades? If that happens, what can be done? Can success be achieved under the current ownership regime "as is"? Or should the organization head in a new direction? What options are available going forward?

Some ideas are presented below. All are feasible, although ownership and/or fans might not consider some of them viable.

Maintain the Status Quo

One option, and it's the outcome that's most likely to occur because it's the one that almost every NFL team follows, is to hire head coaches and general managers and if they don't produce a winning team then fire them and hire a replacement. At some point along the way the franchise might get lucky and find personnel with the formula that produces a winning team.

This template has resulted in the Lions' revolving door through which twenty head coaches have passed since Bill Ford bought the team in the 1960s.[212] The number of general managers is less because Ford employed two (Russ Thomas and Matt Millen) that were failures but were kept around for years because Ford liked them.

Bill Ford passed away in 2014 at which time control of the team passed to his widow Martha Firestone Ford. She ran the team until 2020 when she handed it off to her daughter Sheila Ford Hamp. It was Hamp who fired Matt Patricia and Bob Quinn and hired Head Coach Dan Campbell and General Manager Brad Holmes. Lions' fans are understandably jaded about the Ford family's skills in running the team and their displeasure was displayed in 2021 when they mercilessly booed Hamp while she spoke during a ceremony at Ford Field honoring Hall of Famer Calvin Johnson.

Hamp represents a new generation of Lions' ownership. She walked into a difficult situation and her attempt to fix it will take time. Perhaps she'll fail, but there's also a chance she'll succeed. Maybe she pushed the right buttons in hiring Campbell and Holmes. Time will tell, but in the meantime Lions' fans remain skeptical.

Just because the same family owns a team for many years doesn't mean the team's fortunes become carved in stone. Consider the Pittsburgh Steelers. They joined the NFL in 1933 (as the Pittsburgh Pirates—they became the Steelers in 1940) and were owned by a man named Art Rooney. For decades the Steelers were a second-tier team that earned one playoff appearance during their first thirty-seven years in the league.[213] Rooney ran it on a tight budget from necessity not choice and relied heavily on local talent to fill the team's roster. Then, in 1969, Rooney hired an assistant coach from the Baltimore Colts named Chuck Noll.[214] Noll was appointed head coach of the Steelers and placed in charge of draft choices. He turned out to be a genius at both jobs and within a few years turned the Pittsburgh Steelers into a top-tier team. They won their division in 1972, and the 1974 Super Bowl. In the 1974 draft he did something no one else has accomplished before or since: he selected four future Hall of Famers. The Steelers won four Super Bowls under Noll and have been a top team since. They've had down years along the way, but have been able to bounce back and contend. Thus, Noll not only turned the Steelers into a great team, he also instituted a system and culture that allowed the Steelers to stay near or at the top long after he departed the scene. The Rooney family still owns the franchise which is now run by Art's grandson, Art Rooney II. A hallmark of the team since Noll's day has been organizational stability. It's incredible but true that from 1969-2022 the Steelers have had a grand total of three head coaches.

The point here is it's possible that current Lions' ownership can turn things around the way they the Rooneys did in Pittsburgh, but it would require hiring the right head coach/GM combination. It may not be likely, but it's possible.

Over the years, many Lions' fans have expressed their wish that the Fords sell the team. The thinking is that new ownership might be the answer. Perhaps that's true, but an ownership change is not likely. NFL teams rarely change hands these days and there are a few reasons why. One is the price: depending on the team, NFL franchises are worth $2-$3 billion which means there are very few people who can afford to buy one. In fact, some observers think the NFL's future is corporate ownership of teams because business organizations are better able than individuals to raise the financial capital to meet the purchase price. Partnerships can buy teams, but the problem with this form of ownership is that there are often disputes among the partners. (This is one of the reasons Bill Ford bought out the other Lions' partners in the 1960s.) Another reason why teams rarely change hands is because they are so lucrative. An NFL team is a figurative gold mine: the salary cap amount for the players is roughly equal to each team's annual television revenue. Put fans in the stands, sell them hot dogs, peanuts, beer, and souvenirs which should easily cover your stadium lease, coaches and front office operation…you don't have to be a business genius to earn major profits owning an NFL team. This high profitability is why teams have become so valuable. Remember that Bill Ford paid $4.5 million for the Lions when the deal was consummated in 1964. The franchise is currently valued at about $2 billion. Thus, if the Fords sold the Lions they would be exposed to an enormous capital gain that is potentially taxable. The capital gain is the difference between the sale price (let's use $2 billion) and the cost basis ($4.5 million plus costs incurred by the Lions that have increased the value of the team) which would be a very large amount. The capital gains tax rate on a transaction of that size is currently 20 percent which means the tax bill could be huge. This is another reason why NFL teams don't change hands often, especially teams that have been in the same family for years. The tax consequences of selling are enormous.

Maintaining the status quo is the high-probability outcome. Hopefully, the team has found, or will soon find, a Chuck Noll.

Hire a Strongman

Lions fans have sometimes wondered why the team doesn't hire a strongman with a proven record of success. A Vince Lombardi/Chuck Noll/Bill Parcells/Bill Walsh/Bill Belichick type, someone who turned around a moribund team and took it to multiple Super Bowls. Hire them, give them control, and see what happens.

There are a few problems with this approach. First and foremost, it's easier said than done because there just aren't many people out there who fit the job description. Furthermore, those that do fit the description *and are available* don't come cheap. For all the NFL head coaches that have been hired over the last several decades, only a tiny handful have won multiple championships. The ones who have accomplished this are so valuable that the teams they're associated with usually pay major money to keep them.

The Lions attempted this approach, first in the 1970s when they hired Don McCafferty and then again in the 1990s with Bobby Ross. Neither coach worked out. McCafferty died of a heart attack during training camp of his second season with the Lions, and Ross left Detroit with health problems and frustrated that he couldn't change the team's culture. The team also gave major control to Joe Schmidt, Monte Clark, and Matt Millen. But Schmidt and Clark were hampered by Russ Thomas killing players' morale with his tightwad ways, and Matt Millen turned out to be a horrible football team manager.

The proven-strongman approach is an option but don't hold your breath waiting for it to happen. The more likely outcome is the Ford family continues to hire and fire coaches and general managers, hoping they'll find ones with the formula for success.

The Expansion Team Approach

Another strategy the Lions could consider is the expansion team approach. This is a radical plan where Lions' ownership throws up their hands and declares that the team is cursed. The only way to turn around the organization is to exorcise the demons and make a new beginning.

This proposal requires a complete, total organizational housecleaning. The ownership is unlikely to change for the reasons stated earlier, but everything else changes. Fire all the employees—*every single one of them*—and start fresh. Release or trade every player, fire every front office type, fire the custodians and groundkeepers. Everybody goes. Have a demolition company destroy the team's Allen Park headquarters, sell the land, and build a new building somewhere else. Make a complete, total, fresh beginning. And while they're at it, move to an outdoor stadium so they're better able to play in the elements. Abandon Ford Field, or at least remove the roof.

If the Lions don't want to tear down buildings or leave Ford Field, they could employ a strategy used by the once-hapless Chicago Cubs. The team brought a Greek Orthodox priest to Wrigley Field who sprayed holy water around the Cubs' dugout. The Lions could do something similar: there must be many Detroit area ministers and mullahs and priests and rabbis who are Lions' fans and want to help the team.[215] The Lions could go a step further. Remember the famous foul ball in Game 6 of the Cubs/Marlins 2003 National League Championship Series? The one that Cubs' fan Steve Bartman tried to snare, which may have prevented Cubs' outfielder Mosies Alou from making the catch? The play that completely turned around the game and series and landed the Marlins in the World Series instead of the Cubs? Chicago's Harry Carey Restaurant Group bought that baseball at auction and had a Hollywood special effects expert blow it up before thousands of Cubs' fans during spring training in Arizona in 2004. To carry out this strategy the Lions would need to obtain certain items: a few that come to mind are the penalty flag that was thrown and then picked up in Dallas in 2015; the ball that Eddie Murray pushed wide-right in San Francisco in 1983; Justin Tucker's kicking shoe (they'll never get Tom Dempsey's). Many Lions' fans would be willing to help compile the list and acquire the items. And then, in a fantastic ceremony before tens of thousands of fans, destroy the cursed things. This would allow the Lions to have a new beginning.

The strategy helped the Cubs: they finally won the World Series in 2016. It might work for the Lions. Could the outcome be worse than what Lions' fans have seen during the last sixty-plus years?

Let the Fans Help

Lions' fans have become jaded over the years, to the point of becoming highly cynical of their team. Perhaps it's time to allow the fans to put up or shut up. Offer fans the opportunity to manage the team.

This idea was given a one-game trial in major league baseball many years ago. In the early 1950s a man named Bill Veeck bought the St. Louis Browns (today's Baltimore Orioles). The Browns were poor cousins to the more popular Cardinals so Veeck did things to stimulate interest in his team. He once sent up to bat (against the Detroit Tigers) 3'7" tall Eddie Gaedel. In his only appearance in a game, Gaedel—wearing uniform #1/8—drew a walk. He went to first base and was immediately pulled for a pinch runner.

A few days later (on August 24, 1951) in a game against the Philadelphia Athletics (today's Oakland A's) the Browns held Grandstand Managers Night. Over a thousand fans were chosen in advance, seated together in the stands, and given two signs: one reading "Yes" and the other "No." At various times the game, they were asked what the team should do. A man facing the fans held up signs asking questions such as "shall we bunt?", "shall we steal?", "infield back?", and for pitchers in trouble, "shall we yank him?" Fans raised their signs to vote yes or no and a quick count was made to determine which decision won out. The team followed the fans' instructions and won the game 5-3.

Modern technology would allow today's version of fan management to look much different. Lions' fans could vote electronically—choosing offensive plays, defensive plays, player substitutions, kickoff vs onside kick, punt vs fake punt, etcetera—and their decisions would be transmitted to the field almost instantaneously. Furthermore, there is a savvy group of fans out there who would be involved: those who grew up playing Madden NFL. The game made its debut in 1988 and well over a hundred million copies have been sold. We are now in our second generation of football gamers familiar with NFL play-calling. Gamers could design plays and make the Lions' field decisions. Bold innovation might result. And why couldn't fans choose draft picks and free agents? It's unlikely they would expend three consecutive first-round picks on wide receivers.

Again, could the outcome be worse than what the Lions have produced over the last several years? If nothing else, current Lions' ownership/management might embrace it as a way to get the fans off their backs. If fans ran the team and produced poor results, who would they have to blame but themselves?

Rebrand as Loveable Losers

The Lions might consider borrowing another idea from the Chicago Cubs' playbook: admit the team is not going to win and rebrand as loveable losers. The Cubs rode this formula to financial success for years. Fans went to the games in droves, not expecting to see their team win but enjoying the experience nonetheless. They were having fun watching their loveable losers, the Chicago Cubs.

The Lions could take this approach, although in the hypercompetitive NFL it's not certain Detroit fans would embrace it. Here's the formula: stop talking about Super Bowls, forget about making the playoffs, and instead hire a marketing consulting company to develop a business strategy for branding the Detroit Lions as loveable losers. Just imagine: no longer would Lions' fans curse their team, carry signs, and wear paper bags over their heads. No more angry fan parades and general managers hanged in effigy. Instead, when the Lions fumble the ball at key moments during a game or allow opponents' receivers to run free in the end zone, fans would laugh and say, "Oh, those Lions! They've gone and done it again!"

This strategy would be more effective if the team changed its name and adopted a new logo. Get rid of the fierce lion leaping for its prey. Instead, make the team's symbol a happy little baby lion. Fans at Ford Field would no longer roar before kickoffs, they'd meow. The name Detroit Kittens seems too tame, but opponents might not know that a lion kitten can also be called a whelp. So, let's go with the Detroit Whelps.

<h1 align="center">Endnotes</h1>

[1] The first Super Bowl was played at the end of the 1966 season. Prior to that, the ultimate game of the season was the NFL Championship Game which pitted the winner of the Eastern Conference against the winner of the Western Conference.

[2] HOF = member of the Professional Football Hall of Fame in Canton, Ohio.

[3] See Jerry Green, *Detroit Lions* (New York: Macmillan Publishing, 1973), and Charlie Sanders and Larry Paladino, *Tales from the Detroit Lions* (Champaign, IL: Sports Publishing, 2005).

[4] George Richards sold the team to Fred Mandel in 1940. Mandel sold the team in 1948.

[5] An excellent source on the Lions' first four-plus decades is Jerry Green's book *Detroit Lions* (New York: Macmillan Publishing, 1973).

[6] Parker had been a fullback on the Lions' 1935 championship team.

[7] Briggs Stadium was renamed Tiger Stadium in 1961. Coverage of these games here is brief because the Lions dynasty era is not the focus of this book. Jerry Green's (1973) book has the details of individual games. The 1952 season is the subject an article by Doug Warren, "1952: The Dawning of Motown's Gridiron Empire." *The Coffin Corner* Vol. 25, no. 5 (2004). https://docslib.org/doc/10920230/1952-the-dawning-of-motowns-gridiron-empire, accessed 29 April 2023.

Richard Bak has written an excellent book on the Lions' 1950s dynasty teams. See Richard Bak, *When Lions were Kings: The Detroit Lions and the Fabulous Fifties* (Detroit: Wayne State University Press, 2020).

[8] According to Joe Schmidt, Bobby Layne was the X-Factor during the Lions' dynasty era. As far as Layne was concerned, everything was about winning and the team. If Layne thought a player was hurting the cause he'd tell Coach Buddy Parker to pull the offender from the game and send in a replacement, and Parker would do it. Telephone interview with Joe Schmidt, November 6, 2019.

[9] It may seem strange that NFL players were being drafted and serving in the military, but that's the way it was at the time. The military draft was in force, and few deferments were approved. In 1958, at the height of his career, Elvis Presley was drafted and served in the US Army.

[10] See Bob Braunwart and Bob Carroll, "The Mugging of Bobby Layne." *The Coffin Corner* Vol. 2, no. 12 (1980). https://www.profootballresearchers.com/coffin-corner80s/02-12-048.pdf, accessed 29 April 2023.

[11] According to Jerry Green, the buyout of McMillin's contract when the Lions promoted Parker to head coach is the reason why the Lions' owners were so reluctant to offer Parker contracts longer than one-year in duration. They didn't want to ever again fire a coach and then have to pay him for not coaching. Jerry Green, *Detroit Lions* (New York: Macmillan Publishing, 1973), page 18.

[12] Jerry Green, *Detroit Lions* (New York: Macmillan Publishing, 1973), page 38.

[13] See "Coach Shocks Banquet," *Detroit Free Press*, August 13, 1957, and "When a Bellboy's Error Shook Up Detroit Lions," *Detroit Free Press*, May 20, 1976.

[14] In calculating winning percentage, the NFL treats a tie game as ½ of a win, and ½ of a loss.

[15] The Vikings have never won a Super Bowl, but based on division titles they've been the most successful team in the NFC Central/North.

[16] The 1-12 record is from 1958-2020. Strictly speaking, the Lions have played in more than thirteen playoff games since 1957. During the 1960s the NFL staged the Playoff Bowl—disdainfully called the "Toilet Bowl"—which was an essentially meaningless game between the two runner ups to determine third and fourth place standings. See Don Shipley, "The NFL Playoff Bowl: A Bittersweet Trip in the 1960s." *The Coffin Corner* Vol 44, no. 1 (2022), pp. 13-17. The Lions played in the first three Playoff Bowls (1960-1962) and won all three. Their 1-12 playoff record refers to playoff games in the format where a win advances the team toward the championship.

[17] Their third Divisional Championship was in 1983. There was only one wild card team then, so the Lions received a first round bye. The wild card winner played the top seed in the second round. The Lions were the #3 seed so they played on the road against #2 seed San Francisco.

[18] For the story of Anderson and Fife's falling out and William Clay Ford's ascendency see "New masters in the den of Lions." *Sports Illustrated*, February 6, 1961, pp. 44-46. https://vault.si.com/vault/1961/02/06/new-masters-in-the-den-of-lions, accessed 29 April 2023.

[19] David Harris. *The Genius: How Bill Walsh Reinvented Football and Created a Dynasty* (New York: Random House, 2008).

[20] The twenty-three losses came over twenty-two years because in 1994 the Lions played twice in Green Bay, a regular season game and a playoff game.

[21] Earl Morrall, who played at Michigan State, had an eventful twenty-one-year career in the NFL. He is best known for (1) being the starting quarterback for the Baltimore Colts in Super Bowl III which the Colts lost to the NY Jets, (2) coming off the bench in Super Bowl V to lead the Colts to victory over the Dallas Cowboys, and (3) being the number two quarterback on the 1972 perfect-season Miami Dolphins. When starter Bob Griese went down with an injury, Morrall stepped in and quarterbacked the Dolphins to eleven of their seventeen wins.

[22] Incredibly, Lombardi's five championships occurred over a seven-year span.

[23] For a detailed discussion of the 1962 Lions, see Jerry Green, *Detroit Lions* (New York: McMillin and Company, 1973), pp. 70-74.

[24] See Jerry Green, *Detroit Lions* (McMillin Publishing Co., 1973), pp. 70-74, and Doug Warren, "11-3 and Forever Second." *The Coffin Corner* Vol. 26, no. 4 (2004). http://www.profootballresearchers.org/archives/Website_Files/Coffin_Corner/26-06-1051.pdf, accessed 29 April 2023.

[25] "Wilson Takes the Blame: I Called Play." *Detroit Free Press*, October 8, 1962.

[26] Green (1973, p. 74). Green says the failed pass play caused a schism between the Lions' offensive and defensive units that lasted for years. Plimpton (1966) says that for several games afterwards when the defense was leaving the field and the offense was coming on, Schmidt would sarcastically say to Plum as they were passing, "Pass, Milt, three times and then punt." See George Plimpton, *The Paper Lion: Confessions of a Last-String Quarterback* (New York: Little, Brown and Co., 1966).

[27] Thomas is the subject of Chapter 3. He and Schmidt had a testy relationship.

[28] Jerry Green (1973, p. 178) says that Schmidt didn't want to draft Landry, but was overruled by owner Ford and GM Thomas. Bobby Layne recommended Landry to the Lions.

[29] "It's Sad Ending…Lions Lose." *Detroit Free Press*, December 27, 1970.

[30] David Harris, *The Genius: How Bill Walsh Reinvented Football and Created a Dynasty*. (New York: Random House, 2008), chapter 2.

[31] San Francisco had an identical 2-14 record, but the Lions were judged worse because their 1979 opponents had a .520 winning record while the 49ers opponents' record was .527. "IU Plan: Get Wilson, Win Bowl." *Florida Today*, December 21, 1979.

[32] "Clark takes loss with grim humor." *Detroit Free Press*, October 3, 1983.

[33] "Lions' victory grants Clark a stay of rumored execution." *Detroit Free Press*, October 10, 1983.

[34] "Lions blast the Pack, 38-14." *Detroit Free Press*, October 10, 1983.

[35] "Murray can kick himself for the one that got away." *Detroit Free Press*, January 1, 1984.

[36] "Murray can kick himself for the one that got away." *Detroit Free Press*, January 1, 1984.

[37] "Post-game: Regrets, sadness." *Detroit Free Press*, January 1, 1984.

[38] Keith Dorney, *Black and Honolulu Blue: In the Trenches of the NFL* (Chicago: Triumph Books, 2003).

[39] One thing Clark did accomplish was beating Minnesota with greater frequency than his predecessors. Clark's Lions teams were 5-8 against the Vikings.

[40] Player contract demands were a problem during the Clark era, but they involved General Manager Russ Thomas, not Clark. This issue is discussed in Chapter 3. Turnover among assistant coaches was another issue during the Clark years.

[41] GM Russ Thomas retired on December 26, 1989 and was replaced by Chuck Schmidt.

[42] The Lions had high expectations for Ware because he'd been successful quarterbacking the Run and Shoot at the University of Houston. However, his career in Detroit never took off.

[43] "N.F.L. '90; See How They Run and Shoot." *New York Times*, September 2, 1990. https://www.nytimes.com/1990/09/02/sports/nfl-90-see-how-they-run-and-shoot.html, accessed 29 April 2023.

[44] The Run and Shoot has morphed into various versions over the years. It's often called the Spread Offense.

[45] "N.F.L. '90; See How They Run and Shoot." *New York Times*, September 2, 1990. https://www.nytimes.com/1990/09/02/sports/nfl-90-see-how-they-run-and-shoot.html, accessed 29 April 2023.

[46] "Kramer gets his shot in the Run-And-Shoot." *The Washington Post*, January 8, 1992.

[47] Barry Sanders and Mark E. McCormick. *Barry Sanders: Now You See Him* (Emmis Books, 2003).

[48] They say imitation is the most sincere form of flattery. The Lions' success in scoring points drew attention; the Houston Oilers, Atlanta Falcons, and Seattle Seahawks—dome teams like the Lions—began using the four-receiver offense.

[49] "Memory of loss lingers for Lions." *Detroit Free Press*, September 1, 1991.

[50] Matthews was back in the lineup late in the season.

[51] Some of these numbers were displayed by CBS Television at the start of the Detroit/Dallas divisional playoff game. Thanks to Jon Hamilton for reproducing them. https://thewarmtake.com/my-1991-detroit-lions-history-lesson/ The indoor giveaway/takeaway number that CBS provided is incorrect according to the data from Pro Football Reference. That data set says the Lions were +19 indoors which is reported here.

[52] Takeaway/Giveaway is the number of fumbles recovered plus interceptions by the Lions minus the number of fumbles lost and interceptions thrown by the Lions.

[53] "For 50 years, he has been…The Lion King." *Detroit Free Press*, November 3, 2013.

[54] John U. Bacon. "Owner retains his integrity but misses Super Bowl Glory." *The Detroit News*, December 22, 1996. Bill's brother Benson also took to the bottle; Bill was able to quit drinking, but Benson was not.

[55] The Anderson/Fife saga dated to the late 1940s and included alleged lying, backstabbing, and a messy divorce. For details, see Tex Maule, "New Masters in the Den of Lions." *Sports Illustrated*, February 6, 1961. https://vault.si.com/vault/1961/02/06/new-masters-in-the-den-of-lions, accessed 29 April 2023.

[56] Back in those days the draft was held at the end of the calendar year for the upcoming season. Thus, the 1960 draft was held in 1959.

[57] "Anderson Hanged in Effigy by Lions." *Detroit Free Press*, December 16, 1961. The Lions drafted and lost Fred Biletnikoff (HOF) to the AFL in 1965.

[58] In January 1961, Ford told the *Detroit Free Press* he was appointed to the board before he had an ownership stake. See "Just-a-GM Anderson Is Still 'On His Own.'" *Detroit Free Press*, January 25, 1961.

[59] Randy Snow. "Ten Things You Probably Don't Know about the Detroit Lions." *The Coffin Corner* Vol 43, no. 3 (2021).

[60] Some sources say Ford paid $4.5 million while others say he paid $6.0 million. It's also not clear how much he paid for his minority stake prior to purchasing the remaining shares. Another item that is unclear is how many shareholders there were when Ford bought them all out. Most sources say there were 140-plus, but in an interview in 1988, Ford said there were 250. See "William Clay Ford: The dean of Detroit Owners 'grew up' with the Lions." *Detroit Free Press*, June 30, 1988. The Lions are now worth over $2 billion.

[61] Dr. Jerry Argovitz and J. David Miller. *Super Agent: The One Book the NFL & NCAA Don't Want You to Read* (New York: Sports Publishing, 2013). Argovitz became involved in a major lawsuit involving the Lions and Billy Sims.

[62] Bacon (1996), op. cit.

[63] Author interview with Joe Schmidt, 11/6/19. Schmidt did praise Thomas for doing well in helping select draft choices. One person who said nice things about Thomas was Charlie Sanders. Once, when Sanders was having financial problems, Thomas emptied his pockets for Sanders so he could buy Christmas presents for his children.

[64] Judy Barrista. "Automaker William Clay Ford Sr. couldn't make Lions hum." NFL.com March 9, 2014. https://www.nfl.com/news/automaker-william-clay-ford-sr-couldn-t-make-lions-hum-0ap2000000332257, accessed 29 April 2023.

[65] Author interview with Jerry Green, September 12, 2020.

[66] "Getting to know the Lions." *Detroit Free Press*, February 7, 1985.

[67] There were free agents but they were not top-shelf players because they were undrafted or had been released by their team.

[68] For descriptions of how the systems worked, see Michael Schottey, "How Free Agency Changed the NFL Forever," BleacherReport.com, 2013, https://bleacherreport.com/articles/1561856-how-free-agency-changed-the-nfl-forever, accessed 29 April 2023.

Anthony Cosenza, "A History Lesson on NFL Free Agency: Remember 'Plan B Free Agency?'" Cincyjungle.com, 2013. https://www.cincyjungle.com/2013/3/5/4065394/a-history-lesson-on-2013-nfl-free-agency-remember-plan-b-free-agency, accessed 29 April 2023.

[69] Author interview with Joe Schmidt, November 6, 2019.

[70] According to news reports, the 2021 contract is worth $110 billion over eleven years. This works out to $110 billion/11 years/32 teams = $312 million per year per team.

[71] "Notes from camp: Lions give Bubba longer contract." *Detroit Free Press*, July 18, 1980.

[72] "Lion walkout Baker: 'Take it all the way.'" *Detroit Free Press*, August 9, 1980.

[73] "Pact spats split Lions' camp." *Detroit Free Press*, August 8, 1980.

[74] Overpaid players can damage morale too. Younger players might resent being out-earned by older players with diminished skills, especially if the salary gap is wide. This is a reason why some teams are ruthless about getting rid of veterans.

[75] Dr. Jerry Argovitz and J. David Miller. *Super Agent: The One Book the NFL & NCAA Don't Want You to Read* (New York: Sports Publishing, 2013).

[76] Argovitz and Miller, 2013.

[77] "William Clay Ford: The dean of Detroit owners 'grew up' with the Lions." *Detroit Free Press*, June 30, 1988.

[78] The others were Don McCafferty who succeeded Schmidt and coached one season before dying of a heart attack in the summer of 1974, and Bobby Ross who resigned in 2000.

[79] "Lions Surprised as Joe Schmidt Resigns." Associated Press, January 13, 1973.

[80] Author interview with Joe Schmidt, November 6, 2019.

[81] Dave Birkett. "For 50 years, he has been…The Lion King." *Detroit Free Press*, November 3, 2013.

[82] "Lions interested in Vainisi." *Detroit Free Press*, February 3, 1987.

[83] "Getting nowhere, Vainisi will be gone." *Detroit Free Press*, December 28, 1989. In his autobiography, Barry Sanders is highly critical of Chuck Schmidt whom he blames for dismantling the 1991 team. See Barry Sanders and Mark E. McCormick, *Barry Sanders: Now You See Him* (Emmis Books, 2003).

[84] "Is I-75 Traffic Best Way to Stop Vikes?" *Detroit Free Press*, September 27, 1976.

[85] "'Automatic' extra point blocked, Lions lose thriller to Vikes, 10-9." *Detroit Free Press*, September 27, 1976.

[86] Today, divisional record is the next tiebreaker after head-to-head matches.

[87] The NFL had experimented with night football before, but it wasn't a regular weekly event until 1970. The

Lions and Packers played a Monday night game at Tiger Stadium in 1964 but it wasn't televised nationally.

[88] "Somebody up there didn't like the Lions?" *Detroit Free Press*, November 13, 1972.

[89] "Somebody up there didn't like the Lions?" *Detroit Free Press*, November 13, 1972.

[90] The 2008 games were memorable too, but those are delayed until Chapter 8 on the 0-16 season of 2008.

[91] "PATsies! Botched snap spoils comeback." *Detroit Free Press*, December 20, 2004.

[92] Muhlbach overcame the setback and went on to serve as the Lions' long-snapper for seventeen seasons.

[93] Marshall was a colorful character with a mixed legacy (discussed later in this chapter). He was also a notorious team meddler, even to the extent of telling the team's captain whether to call heads or tails for the pregame coin flip. See John Eisenberg, *The League: How Five Rivals Created the NFL and Launched a Sports Empire* (New York: Basic Books, 2018).

[94] Hall of Famer Marion Motley is considered one of the greatest football players of all time.

[95] Strode went on to have a notable acting career, playing several memorable roles including the gladiator who fought in the ring against Kirk Douglas in *Spartacus*, and John Wayne's loyal friend Pompey in *The Man Who Shot Liberty Valance*.

[96] Ane was Hawaiian.

[97] At the time, the goal posts were located at the goal line. They're now located at the back of the end zone.

[98] "Skins End Lions' Streak at Six Straight, 18-17." *Detroit Free Press*, November 12, 1956.

[99] George Puscas, "Dumb de dumb dumb – done." *Detroit Free Press*, November 9, 1981.

[100] "You can say I choked: Numb Hanson not used to failing." *Detroit Free Press*, September 21, 1992.

[101] The story of how and why the Lions ended up in Pontiac is described in Jeffrey R. Wing, "Olympic Bids, Professional Sports, and Urban Politics: Four Decades of Stadium Planning in Detroit, 1936-1975" (2016). United States History Commons. Dissertations. 2155. https://ecommons.luc.edu/luc_diss/2155/, accessed 29 April 2023

[102] Close-in parking matters because stadium-controlled parking allows a team/stadium to earn parking revenue. This wasn't the case at Tiger Stadium where game days were an urban parking free-for-all as fans used street parking or paid homeowners and business owners to park on their lawns and in their parking lots.

[103] There were traffic problems involved with the first preseason game but they believed to have been caused by factors that would no longer be issues on opening night. For example, too many fans showed up at one shopping center to park and ride buses to the stadium, and many of the parking spaces at the Silverdome were occupied by construction equipment. See "Lions fans clog up Pontiac." *Detroit Free Press*, August 24, 1975.

[104] "Lions bid not-so-fond farewell." *Detroit Free Press*, January 7, 2002.

[105] The home team had to sell 85 percent of the tickets for the game to be shown locally, but if the team was close to meeting the goal but didn't reach it they could apply for an exemption from the NFL.

[106] Covered field here refers to stadiums with a roof or retractable roof. The latest covered venue is Sofi Stadium in Inglewood, California, the new (2020) home of the Rams and Chargers. It has a covered field, but the sides of the stadium are open to the weather. It's referred to here as a covered stadium which it is, but it's not,

strictly speaking, an indoor stadium.

[107] Until recently, attempts to maintain grass in domed stadiums were very expensive and had mixed results. In recent years, grass has been successfully used in stadiums with retractable roofs.

[108] This statement is not true if the outdoor field is frozen.

[109] Barry Sanders and Mark E. McCormick. *Barry Sanders: Now You See Him* (Emmis Books, 2003), p. 150.

[110] See "Utley blames turf for paralyzing injury." *Detroit Free Press*, March 18, 1992, and "NFLPA asking teams to change all fields to natural grass." Associated Press, December 15, 2020.

[111] The Rams have five Super Bowl appearances (three as a dome team), Colts three appearances (two as dome team), and Falcons have two Super Bowl appearances (both as dome team). While we're on the topic of dome teams and Super Bowls, here's another fact to consider: only two dome teams have ever won an outdoor playoff game during their run to the Super Bowl.

[112] "Dome Football Teams Really Are Worse Playing Outdoors." Probabilis, October 15, 2020. https://probabilis.blogspot.com/2020/10/dome-football-teams-really-are-worse.html, accessed 29 April 2023.

[113] See, for example, "Dome at Home: Advantage or Disadvantage?" Dome at Home: Advantage or Disadvantage? : r/nfl (reddit.com), accessed 29 April 2023.

[114] Due to a dispute over the lease at then Briggs Stadium, the Lions returned to the University of Detroit stadium for the 1940 season. The choice of starting the sample in 1938 is arbitrary.

[115] Readers may criticize these results by saying they compare apples and oranges, that the game of football as played from 1938-1974 was vastly different from what has been played the last few decades so comparing a team's home and road records then with more recent times is a false comparison. It's true that the game has changed significantly over the years, but that doesn't mean it changed the magnitude of home field advantage.

[116] C. Barry Pfitzner, Stephen D. Lang, and Tracy D. Rishel. "The Determinants of Scoring in NFL Games and Beating the Over/Under Line." *New York Economic Review* Vol. 40 (Fall 2009), pp. 28-39. https://econpapers.repec.org/article/nyenyervw/v_3a40_3ay_3a2009_3ai_3a1_3ap_3a28-39.htm, accessed 29 April 2023.

[117] The 1970 playoff loss at Dallas was when the Lions were still an outdoor team.

[118] Hindsight is always twenty-twenty. In 1975 no one knew how occupying a domed stadium would impact a team's record because the only data available were from the Oilers and they'd only been in a dome for a few years.

[119] Domed stadiums also allow Northern cities to host Super Bowls.

[120] "Where has season gone?" *Detroit Free Press*, November 22, 2004.

[121] Amy Kaplan. "Damien Woody says the Lions were the most 'dysfunctional' franchise he ever played for." Fansided.com.

[122] As of 2021, there are eight members of the 2,000-yard club.

[123] Barry Sanders and Mark E. McCormick. *Barry Sanders: Now You See Him* (Emmis Books, 2003).

[124] Barry Sanders and Mark E. McCormick. *Barry Sanders: Now You See Him* (Emmis Books, 2003), p. 128.

[125] "Though a lame duck, Ford Sr finally makes the right move." *Detroit Free Press*, January 10, 2001.

[126] "Though a lame duck, Ford Sr finally makes the right move." *Detroit Free Press*, January 10, 2001.

[127] Millen didn't play in that game. He was a run-stuffing linebacker, and the Washington coaching staff was much more concerned about the Lions' spread-offense passing game. Thus, Millen was deactivated for the game.

[128] Michael Rosenberg. "The Seven-Year Glitch." *Sports Illustrated*, December 2, 2013. https://vault.si.com/vault/2013/12/02/the-sevenyear-glitch, accessed 29 April 2023.

[129] Rosenberg, 2013.

[130] "Schmidt declines new job." *Detroit Free Press*, January 10, 2001.

[131] "Lion's share of blame goes to Millen." *Boston Globe*, December 2, 2006. http://archive.boston.com/sports/football/patriots/articles/2006/12/02/lions_share_of_blame_goes_to_millen/, accessed 29 April 2023.

[132] Author interview with Jerry Green. September 12, 2020.

[133] Jeremy Reisman, "Matt Millen opens up on his time as Lions GM: 'I was in over my head.'" PrideofDetroit.com, 2018. https://www.prideofdetroit.com/2018/5/14/17352418/matt-millen-opens-up-on-his-time-as-lions-gm-i-was-in-over-my-head, accessed 29 April 2023.

[134] "Bill Dow, "How the Detroit Lions drove Joey Harrington into depression; Thanksgiving revenge memories." *Detroit Free Press*, November 24, 2020.

[135] Joey Harrington. "Despite What You May Think, My NFL Career Was a Success." *Sports Illustrated*, December 21, 2015. Harrington describes Millen as "one of the only stand-up guys in [the Lions] organization." https://the-cauldron.com/despite-what-you-may-think-my-nfl-career-was-a-success-179aeca1b1e7, accessed 29 April 2023.

[136] Jeremy Reisman. "Matt Millen opens up on his time as Lions GM: 'I was in over my head.'" PrideofDetroit.com, 2018. https://www.prideofdetroit.com/2018/5/14/17352418/matt-millen-opens-up-on-his-time-as-lions-gm-i-was-in-over-my-head, accessed 29 April 2023.

[137] Reisman, 2018.

[138] The Lions had another first-round pick in 2004 which they acquired in a trade. The selected running back Kevin Jones.

[139] Michael Rosenberg. "The Seven-Yea Glitch." *Sports Illustrated*, December 2, 2013. https://vault.si.com/vault/2013/12/02/the-sevenyear-glitch, accessed 29 April 2023.

[140] The Lions gave up Roy Williams and their 7th round pick in 2009 in exchange for Dallas's 1st, 3rd, and 6th round picks in 2009.

[141] Jeremy Reisman. "Matt Millen opens up on his time as Lions GM: 'I was in over my head'". PrideofDetroit.com, 2018. https://www.prideofdetroit.com/2018/5/14/17352418/matt-millen-opens-up-on-his-time-as-lions-gm-i-was-in-over-my-head, accessed 29 April 2023.

[142] Peter King. "Matt Millen Fights for His Life: 'It's getting Late. We Need a Big Stop.'" *Sports Illustrated*, May 14, 2018. https://www.si.com/nfl/2018/05/14/matt-millen-sick-amyloidosis-detroit-lions-mmqb-peter-king, accessed 29 April 2023.

[143] In later rounds of the 2008 draft the Lions chose defensive lineman Cliff Avril and fullback Jerome Felton, both of whom later reached the Pro-Bowl.

[144] Calvin Johnson was a rookie when Millen was fired.

[145] "Doomed to fail? Sadly, Millen was a man without a plan." *Detroit Free Press*, September 25, 2008.

[146] Data are from Spotrac.com/NFL/positional

[147] The Lions' record for catches in a game is 14 by Calvin Johnson against Dallas on October 27, 2013.

[148] "Anti-Millen signs rev up crowd." *Detroit Free Press*, December 5, 2005.

[149] Jeremy Reisman. "Matt Millen opens up on his time as Lions GM: 'I was in over my head.'" PrideofDetroit.com, 2018. https://www.prideofdetroit.com/2018/5/14/17352418/matt-millen-opens-up-on-his-time-as-lions-gm-i-was-in-over-my-head, accessed 29 April 2023.

[150] See John Eisenberg, *The League: How Five Rivals Created the NFL and Launched a Sports Empire* (New York: Basic Books, 2018).

[151] Due to severe roster depletion, the 1944 Chicago Cardinals and Pittsburgh Steelers were temporarily merged into Card/Pitt.

[152] The 16-game season was in place from 1978-2020, the 17-game season went into effect in 2021.

[153] Michael Rosenberg. "Calvin Johnson Doesn't Regret a Thing." *Sports Illustrated*, September 20, 2019. https://www.si.com/nfl/2019/09/20/calvin-johnson-lions-big-interview, accessed 29 April 2023.

[154] See "Balanced 49ers send Lions to 0-3 start." *Detroit Free Press*, September 22, 2008.

[155] "Orlovsky red-faced, but confident." *Detroit Free Press*, October 13, 2008.

[156] "Uncalled for: Late flag gives Vikings new life, crushes Lions' hopes." *Detroit Free Press*, October 13, 2008.

[157] On October 14th, wide receiver Roy Williams was traded to Dallas.

[158] On a sad note, on March 1, 2009 defensive lineman Corey Smith, whose Lions' contract expired at the end of the 2008 season, died in a boating accident off the Florida Gulf Coast. The Lions retired his #93 for the 2009 season.

[159] "Coach did what now?" *Detroit Free Press*, December 31, 2013.

[160] "Mayhew deluged with pro-Caldwell calls." *Detroit Free Press*, January 18, 2014.

[161] The Lions drafted tight end Eric Ebron in the first round. In doing so they passed on Aaron Donald and Odell Beckham. Linebacker Kyle Van Noy was their second-round pick.

[162] While serving as interim head coach, Bevell had to sit out a game because of the COVID virus. Robert Prince served as acting-interim head coach which means that, technically speaking, the Lions had three head coaches during the 2020 season.

[163] "Owner on why the Lions fired Patricia, Quinn: 'It clearly wasn't working.'" *Detroit Free Press*, November 29, 2020.

[164] Shawn Windsor. "Lions owner keeps her promise to fans, but can she find combo that can win?" *Detroit Free*

Press, November 29, 2020.

[165] Campbell considers his mentors to be Bill Parcells and Sean Payton.

[166] See, for example, Mitch Albom, "Empty words from ownership not enough for fans this time." *Detroit Free Press*, January 21, 2021.

[167] "Lions cut rookie cut up." *Detroit Free Press*, August 6, 1963.

[168] Pat Harmon. "The Paper Lion at Boca Raton." *Cincinnati Post and Times Star*, March 19, 1968.

[169] "Paper Lion back on big screen 50 years later." *Detroit Free Press*, April 14, 2018.

[170] One memorable Plimpton movie performance is in the western Rio Lobo. He enters a room brandishing a rifle and delivers his line: "I got a warrant right here sheriff." John Wayne then grabs the rifle from Plimpton's hands and bashes him in the face with it. Moments later Plimpton is shot dead by one of Wayne's allies.

[171] Beamon's record was finally broken in 1991 when US jumper Mike Powell bested it by 2 inches. As of 2022, Powell's jump is still the world record.

[172] Peter Finney, "Tom Dempsey's 63-yard field goal ranks among greatest memories in New Orleans Saints history." *Times-Picayune*, November 8, 2010.

[173] Jake Rossen, "Remembering Tom Dempsey, the Toeless NFL Kicker who Set a 43-Year Field Goal Record." www.mentalfloss.com. https://www.mentalfloss.com/article/598356/tom-dempsey-toeless-nfl-kicker-breaks-record-1970, accessed 29 April 2023.

[174] Author interview with Joe Schmidt, November 6, 2019.

[175] NFL Films, *New Orleans Saints*.

[176] Author interview with Joe Schmidt, November 6, 2019.

[177] Dallas Cowboy's GM Tex Schramm protested Dempsey's squared-off shoe, claiming it gave him an unfair advantage. However, physicists quickly pointed out that the shape of the shoe did not influence the distance the ball traveled. NFL Commissioner Pete Rozelle ordered Schramm to apologize to Dempsey.

[178] The Professional Football Hall of Fame in Canton has one of Dempsey's shoes, but not the one he was wearing when he kicked the record-breaking field goal. Dempsey's kick eventually resulted in the NFL imposing the Tom Dempsey Rule (1977) which says that "any shoe that is worn by a player with an artificial limb on his kicking leg must have a kicking surface that conforms to that of a normal kicking shoe."

[179] "Hughes died of artery disease." *Detroit Free Press*, October 26, 1971.

[180] "He grabbed at his chest, then fell flat." *Detroit Free Press*, October 25, 1971.

[181] https://www.detroitlions.com, accessed 29 April 2023.

[182] "Remembering tragic day Lions' WR Hughes died on field 50 years ago." *Detroit Free Press*, October 24, 2021. Much has been written about Hughes's death. See also Denis M. Crawford, "The Death of Chuck Hughes and Its Impact on NFL Medicine." *The Coffin Corner*, Vol. 43, no. 5 (2021), pp. 10-14.

[183] In the 1930s they moved the goalposts from the back of the end zone to the goal line to make the game more exciting. In 1974, they returned the goalposts to the back of the end zone to make the game more exciting. The difference was in the early days games were low scoring, so moving the goalposts closer would result in

more field goals and thus more points scored. However, by the 1970s the field goal kickers had become so accurate that the idea was to reduce the number of long-range field goals. Also, goalposts at the goal line were a serious safety hazard—many players were injured running into them.

[184] "Catch 22? The Lions just couldn't." *Detroit Free Press*, November 28, 1980.

[185] "Bears swipe Lions' feast in OT, 23-17." *Detroit Free Press*, November 28, 1980.

[186] The NFL has since fiddled with the overtime rules. The big changes are that the overtime period was reduced from 15:00 to 10:00, and if the team with the first possession kicks a field goal, the other team gets a chance on offense. However, if the team with the first possession scores a touchdown the game is over. In 2022 the rules for postseason games were changed so that if one team scores a touchdown on their first possession, the other team also gets a possession.

[187] Kickoffs were moved back to the 35-yard line in 2011.

[188] *2012 NFL Fact and Record Book.*

[189] "Brain freeze helps Bears break the ice." *Chicago Tribune*, November 25, 2002. https://www.chicagotribune.com/news/ct-xpm-2002-11-25-0211250155-story.html, accessed 29 April 2023.

[190] "Bad ending leaves Lions quietly angry." *Detroit Free Press*, November 25, 2002.

[191] "Miller sharp off bench; Edinger boots winner." *Chicago Tribune*, November 25, 2002.

[192] "Miller sharp off bench; Edinger boots winner." *Chicago Tribune*, November 25, 2002.

[193] "Brain freeze helps Bears break the ice." *Chicago Tribune*, November 25, 2002. https://www.chicagotribune.com/news/ct-xpm-2002-11-25-0211250155-story.html, accessed 29 April 2023.

[194] See, for example, Drew Sharp, "Blown chance shows coach is an airhead." *Detroit Free Press*, November 25, 2002.

[195] The 1932 Chicago/Portsmouth game was the NFL's first indoor game. See Doc Emrick, "Doc Emrick tells the odd tale of the 1932 NFL Championship Game." NBC Sports, December 12, 2021.

[196] The Belichick Rule exists because the Patriots were caught filming opponents' coaches' hand signals on the sideline.

[197] "Late end-zone call should not have mattered." *Detroit Free Press*, September 13, 2010.

[198] "Lions lose QB, then game; accept ruling on call." *Detroit Free Press*, September 13, 2010.

[199] Mitch Albom, "Your eyes don't lie: Johnson clearly made a game-winning catch." *Detroit Free Press*, September 13, 2010.

[200] "What others said about it." *Detroit Free Press*, September 13, 2010.

[201] Thanksgiving Day games were not scheduled during WWII.

[202] "Schwartz blows his cool on Forsett TD, but team blows several chances to win." *Detroit Free Press*, November 23, 2012.

[203] "Schwartz blows his cool on Forsett TD, but team blows several chances to win." *Detroit Free Press*, November 23, 2012.

[204] "Jeff Seidel has a bad taste in his mouth after digesting Detroit's latest loss." *Detroit Free Press*, November 23, 2012.

[205] "Caldwell doesn't buy explanation." *Detroit Free Press*, January 5, 2015,

[206] Drew Sharp. "Detroit's playoff loss goes beyond bad calls." www.thenews-messenger.com https://www.thenews-messenger.com/story/sports/nfl/2015/01/06/detroits-playoff-loss-goes-beyond-bad-calls/21331285/, accessed 29 April 2023.

[207] "Lions fall, 24-20, to Cowboys in 1st round." *Detroit Free Press*, January 5, 2015.

[208] "Lions fall, 24-20, to Cowboys in 1st round." *Detroit Free Press*, January 5, 2015.

[209] "Campbell's timeout gave Ravens a gift, cost Lions." *Detroit Free Press*, September 27, 2021.

[210] "Campbell expects an apology for missed delay-of-game call." *Detroit Free Press*, September 27, 2001.

[211] "Campbell's timeout gave Ravens a gift, cost Lions." *Detroit Free Press*, September 27, 2021.

[212] The number is twenty-one head coaches if we include acting-interim head coach Robert Prince who filled in for one game when interim head coach Darrell Bevell was out due to the COVID virus.

[213] Their playoff appearance was in 1947. Their also appeared in the runner-up Playoff Bowl against the Lions at the end of the 1962 season, but it's not included as a playoff appearance because the game did not lead toward the championship.

[214] Art Rooney's son Dan was primarily responsible for hiring Noll. See John Eisenberg, *The League: How Five Rivals Created the NFL and Launched a Sports Empire* (New York: Basic Books, 2018).

[215] In 2016 Lions' team president Ron Wood said he'd take calls from sports exorcists. "Calling all exorcists: Lions are listening." *The Detroit News*, February 18, 2016. https://www.detroitnews.com/story/sports/nfl/lions/2016/02/18/calling-all-exorcists-lions-listening/80573400/, accessed 29 April 2023.

A Note on Sources

Newspaper articles were accessed through Newspapers.com. Several articles came from *Sports Illustrated*. Another important resource was *The Coffin Corner*, which is the official publication of the Professional Football Researchers Association (PFRA) and an excellent reference on NFL history. The author also conducted telephone interviews with Jerry Green and Joe Schmidt who were most helpful and informative.

The following books were used:

Argovitz, Dr. Jerry, and J. David Miller. *Super Agent: The One Book the NFL & NCAA Don't Want You to Read* (New York: Sports Publishing, 2013).

Bak, Richard. *When Lions were Kings: The Detroit Lions and the Fabulous Fifties* (Detroit: Wayne State University Press, 2020).

Dorney, Keith. *Black and Honolulu Blue: In the Trenches of the NFL* (Chicago: Triumph Books, 2003).

Eisenberg, John. *That First Season: How Vince Lombardi Took the Worst Team in the NFL and Set It on the Path to Glory* (Boston: Houghton Mifflin Harcourt, 2009).

______. *The League: How Five Rivals Created the NFL and Launched a Sports Empire* (New York: Basic Books, 2018).

Geoffreys, Clayton. *Calvin Johnson: The Inspiring Story of One of Football's Greatest Wide Receivers* (Calvintir Books, 2020).

Glauber, Bob. *Guts and Genius: The Story of Three Unlikely Coaches Who Came to Dominate the NFL in the '80s* (New York: Grand Central Publishing, 2018).

Green, Jerry. *Detroit Lions* (New York: MacMillan Publishing Co., 1973).

Harris, David. *The Genius: How Bill Walsh Reinvented Football and Created a Dynasty* (New York: Random House, 2008).

Karras, Alex, with Herb Gluck. *Even Big Guys Cry* (New York: Signet Books, 1977).

Plimpton, George. *Paper Lion: Confessions of a Last-String Quarterback* (Boston: Little, Brown and Co, 1966).

Sanders, Barry, and Mark E. McCormick. *Barry Sanders: Now You See Him* (Emmis Books, 2003).

Sanders, Charlie, and Larry Paladino. *Tales from the Detroit Lions* (Champaign, IL: Sports

Publishing, 2005).

Schaefer, John. *Detroit Lions: A Game-by-Game Guide* (Kindle editions, various year).

Smith, Robert. *Illustrated History of Pro Football* Revised edition. (New York: Grosset & Dunlap, 1977).

St. John, Bob. *Heart of a Lion: The Wild and Wolly Life of Bobby Layne* (Dallas: Taylor Publishing Co, 1991).